New
STANDARD COURSE
Pitman Shorthand

New
STANDARD
COURSE
Pitman Shorthand

Revised and Enlarged Edition

Pitman Publishing Corporation

New York　　　　　　　*Chicago*

Preface

Isaac Pitman published the first edition of his shorthand system in 1837, and this revised and enlarged edition of the *New Standard Course in Pitman Shorthand* is issued to mark the centennial of the publication of the system.

History clearly shows that Isaac Pitman's invention has been the greatest contribution to the art of shorthand writing that the world has ever known. Millions of texts of the system have been purchased, and millions have used the system as a means of earning a livelihood. Today, one hundred years after its invention, it is continuously demonstrated that Isaac Pitman designed a writing instrument which meets the most exacting requirements of the stenographic art. The system stands without an equal for the swift and legible recording of speech. Almost without exception, the reporters of Congresses, Parliaments, Courts, throughout the English speaking world—wherever accurate recording of the proceedings is essential—use Pitmanic shorthand.

DISTINCTIVE FEATURES OF THE SYSTEM

Isaac Pitman published the system after an exhaustive study of the structure of the English language, and the system is the result of his scholarly and scientific analysis. Systems before Pitman, and even systems in use today depend largely upon the memorization of hundreds of special forms and arbitrary abbreviations due to the construction of their underlying principles. In Pitman Shorthand stress is placed upon the rational application of the principles used to represent the sounds occurring in English words, and it may be said that Isaac Pitman turned shorthand writing from an art into a science. Several generations of expert writers and teachers have built improvements upon the foundation laid by Isaac Pitman, with the result that today the Pitman writer knows that the system he uses is an instrument in which he may place the greatest confidence.

Handwriting Motion Inadequate. The consonants of the language are represented by a series of simple strokes, selected to provide the most facile joinings with each other. Because these strokes do not follow the slope of ordinary longhand writing, they can be formed with complete distinctiveness when they are joined together and written with great speed. The purpose of shorthand is to represent letters as briefly and as distinctively as possible. *The adoption of a uniform slope in a shorthand system would result in a confusing similarity of consonants,* and the hand of the writer would be retarded because of the necessity for careful and laborious representation of fine distinctions.

Shading of Consonants. In certain cases consonants are paired because of their similarity of sound. The first consonant in the pair is pronounced lightly (as "S"), and the second consonant in the pair is the corresponding heavy sound (as "Z"). The same stroke is used for both consonants, but for the first consonant a light stroke is written, and the second stroke of the pair is written with a slight pressure of the pen. *This use of shading avoids the necessity of employing different strokes to represent similarly sounded consonants.* If, for instance, half and double length strokes were used to represent these pairs, valuable shorthand abbreviating material would be lost, which in Pitman Shorthand is used to represent the addition of letters and even whole syllables. *The use of shading thus saves time and labor for the shorthand writer and shading in itself involves no extra penmanship.*

Elimination of Vowel Signs. Words are represented by a complete shorthand outline of their consonants. Contractions, or "wordsigns", are few in number. Circles, loops and hooks are used for the representation of frequently occurring and natural combinations of consonants in English words. In the application of this abbreviating material the presence or absence of a vowel is indicated, and it is unnecessary to write signs for the vowel sounds. *Here again the shorthand writer is saved much time and labor.* A series of disjoined vowel signs is provided for insertion where necessary, such as in isolated words, or proper names.

Position Writing. Position writing is a simple and effective device for the indication of vowels. Writing a word above, on, or through the line, according to its first vowel sound, *is another means of expressing sound without actual writing, and it is a device highly prized by the fastest writers.* Generations of the best writers in the world have proved that the most effective means of securing compact, swift, and legible shorthand outlines is through complete representation of the consonants, and that the insertion of the vowel signs is a needless waste of the writer's labor.

SUMMARY

In Pitman Shorthand the amount of actual writing has been reduced to a minimum because of the scientific use of the stenographic abbreviating material. Circles, loops, hooks, halving and doubling are devices used for the representation of syllables, and not for the formation of an alphabet. An adequate skill in shorthand writing is developed through the application of the abbreviating principles of the system. These devices are few in number, and they are easily understood and applied. Writers do not have to resort to such doubtful expedients as memorizing large numbers of specially contracted forms or writing only the first part of words, in order to keep pace with a speaker. They are able to develop their skill in accurate note taking without arbitrary memorization and with a minimum of labor. The simple principles of the system permit its writers to maintain and increase their skill, to their own satisfaction and to the satisfaction of those whose utterances they undertake to record.

Features of the Text

THIS TEXT presents the principles of Pitman Shorthand in a logical arrangement; the material provided for the use of students is arranged psychologically. The principles are stated briefly and simply, and each statement is followed by an adequate amount of application. The work of the teacher will be considerably facilitated by the division of the principles into small units of instruction.

An unusual feature of the text is the wealth of drill material provided for each unit of instruction. The amount of this material far exceeds that appearing in any shorthand text previously issued. The exercises have been so constructed that they are similar in context to the material that is dictated to the students in the later stages of the study of the subject. The development of skill in the reading and writing of these exercises is therefore of great importance, for they provide practice as valuable to the student as the dictation he will receive when the principles have been completed. Realization of this will encourage the student and will stimulate rapid progress. The exercises include a cumulative review of the principles and the short forms.

In the application of the principles a vocabulary of the two thousand commonest words has been used. Less frequently occurring words are used occasionally, however, to provide additional illustrations and to demonstrate, in the exercises, the application of a principle to similar words. These additional words are always well within the student's own vocabulary.

Most of the exercises are in shorthand, as it is felt that constant reading of correct shorthand forms is of the utmost value to the student. Experience indicates that it is advisable as far as possible to prevent students writing or seeing incorrectly written outlines, and for this reason the reading of correctly written shorthand, especially in the early stages, is of much importance. The shorthand plates are also useful for home assignments. Starting with Chapter Nine, longhand test material is included, and the teacher may find it advisable sometimes to dictate an exercise as new matter before it is read from the shorthand plate.

When the book has been completed, the *New Standard Dictation Course, Business Letters for Dictation,* or *The Expert Dictator,* will be found useful for the further development of skill in the writing of shorthand for business purposes. These dictation texts include word lists consisting of the third, fourth, and fifth thousand most frequently used words. Expert shorthand writers read as much printed shorthand literature as possible, in order to acquire an extensive shorthand vocabulary. A wide selection of such literature is available, and *Pitman's Journal*, issued monthly, includes many shorthand pages consisting of useful information for the shorthand writer.

The presentation of the principles and the exercise material in this text have been compiled and edited by John Bryant. The book is the result of close familiarity with the work of hundreds of teachers of wide experience, and the whole-hearted interest of these teachers, combined with their helpful observations and recommendations, have made this presentation possible.

CONTENTS

Introduction

SHORTHAND is the art of representing spoken sounds by signs. Pitman Shorthand provides a sign for every sound heard in English words.

Ordinary longhand spelling is seldom phonetic. Pitman Shorthand is phonetic, that is, words are written exactly as they are sounded, and not according to the ordinary longhand spelling. No letters are used that are not wanted to represent the sound. The following illustrations show how to spell when writing shorthand—

palm	is spelled	*pahm*	*wrought*	is spelled	*rawt*
pale	" "	*pāl*	*coal*	" "	*kōl*
key	" "	*kē*	*tomb*	" "	*toom*

The shorthand characters should be made as neatly and as accurately as possible. The size of the shorthand strokes in this text is a good standard to adopt in your own writing. The signs join readily with one another, and they can be written with great speed when you have practiced them sufficiently. Resist the temptation to sacrifice neatness for speed. Speed in writing will naturally follow the practice of neat and accurate writing.

CHAPTER I

PITMAN SHORTHAND ALPHABET

1. The First Six Consonants

The sounds heard in English words are divided as follows:

> Twenty-four Consonants
> Twelve Vowels
> Four Diphthongs

A shorthand sign is provided for each of these sounds.

The first six consonants are represented by straight strokes written downward:

Letter	Sign	Name	As in
P		pee	pay, ape, up
B		bee	bay, Abe, be
T		tee	Tay, ate, it
D		dee	day, aid, do
CH		chay	chest, etch, which
J		jay	jest, edge, age

The arrows indicate the direction in which the strokes are written. They are never written in any other direction.

NOTE: These consonants form pairs: *p* and *b, t* and *d, ch* and *j.* In each pair a *light* sound is represented by a *light* stroke, and a corresponding *heavy* sound is represented by a *heavier* stroke.

2. Vowel *ā*

Vowels are represented by dots and dashes written alongside the consonant strokes. When a vowel comes *before* a consonant, it is placed *before* the stroke (left side); when a vowel comes *after* a consonant, it is placed *after* the stroke (right side).

The long vowel *ā* is represented by a heavy dot:

＼ *ape* ＼ *pay* ＼ *Abe* ＼ *bay* ⋮ *ate* ⋮ *aid* ⋮ *day* ／ *ag*

Write the consonant stroke first, and then place the vowel sign. Tw
light dashes underneath an outline indicate a proper name.

NOTE: There are three places alongside a stroke in which vowels may be
written—beginning, middle, and end, or, first, second, and third place. The
dot for long *ā* is written in the middle place, and it is therefore called a
"second-place vowel."

3. Joining of Consonants

Consonants are joined without lifting the pen, as in longhand
Begin the second where the first ends, and write the stroke in its prope
direction. Note that the first stroke rests on the line.

＞ *p ch* ＼ *bt* └ *tp* │ *dt* ＜ *ch p* ＼ *bd* └ *dp* ／ *j*

＞ *paid* ＞ *page* ＼ *bait* ＼ *babe* └ *tape* │ *date*

4. Vowel *ĕ*

Short *ĕ* is represented by a light dot, and is a second-place vowel

／ *etch* ／ *edge* ＼ *bet* ＼ *pep* │ *Ted* │ *debt* ／ *je*

Note that the first stroke rests on the line. Write the consonant out
line first, and then place the vowel sign.

5. Short Forms for Common Words

A few very frequently used words, such as *be, it, the, to,* are expressed in shorthand by a single sign. These short forms promote speed
writing, and they should be thoroughly memorized.

＼ *be* │ *it* │ *do* ／ *which* ⋅ *the* ＼ *to* ＼ *two* or *to*

│ *but* ／ *who*

6. Phrasing

As an aid to rapid writing, shorthand words may often be joined. This is called phrasing. Outlines should be phrased only when they join easily and naturally, as shown in the examples throughout this textbook. The first word in a phrase is written in its normal position:

to do   *but which*

A small tick *at the end* of a word represents *the*. The tick is written either upward or downward, whichever forms the sharper angle:

to the   *be the*   *do the*   *which the*   *pay the*

paid the

7. Punctuation

The following special punctuation marks are used in shorthand:

period   question   exclamation   hyphen   dash   parenthesis

Other signs are written as in longhand.

EXERCISE 1

1.
2.
3.
4.
5.
6.
7.
8.
9.
10.
11.
12.

CHAPTER II

8. The Second Group of Consonants

The next four pairs of consonants are curves, and they are written downward:

Letter	Sign	Name	As in	Short Form for
F		ef	few, safe, for	
V		vee	view, save, have	*have*
TH		*ith*	**th**igh, ba**th**, **th**ink	*think*
TH		thee	**th**y, ba**th**e, **th**em	*them*
S		ess	seal, ice, us	
Z		zee	zeal, eyes, was	*was*
SH		ish	she, wish, shall	*shall*
ZH		zhee	measure, treasure, usual	*usual* or *usually*

(a) they   say   fade   faith   shape   bathe   shade

(b) fed   fetch   death   shed   essay

9. Vowels ō and ŭ

Long ō is represented by a heavy dash, and is a second-place vowel:

toe   oat   bow   Joe   foe   oath   so   owes   show   showed   boat   both   vote

Short ŭ is represented by a light dash, and is a second-place vowel:

up   us   tub   touch   Dutch   judge

EXERCISE 2

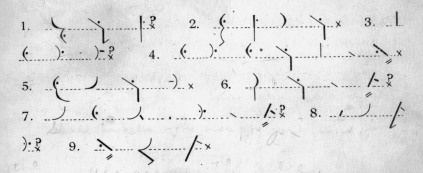

EXERCISE 3

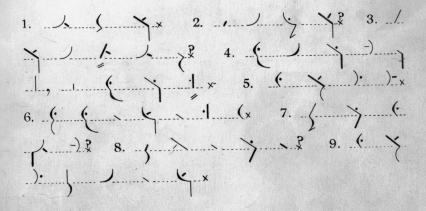

CHAPTER III

10. The Next Eight Consonants

The next eight consonants are all written forward. They are all light strokes except *g* and *ng*:

Letter	Sign	Name	As in	Short Form for
K		kay	cane, leak, come	*come*
G		gay	gain, league, give	*give* or *given*
M		em	may, seem, him	*him*
N		en	nay, seen, no	
NG		ing	long, sing, thing	*thing*
L		el	lay, coal, will	
W		way	weigh, aware, we	*we*
Y		yay	youth, yellow, yes	

When a vowel comes *before* a horizontal stroke it is written *above* the stroke; when a vowel comes *after* a horizontal stroke it is written *below* the stroke.

(*a*) ache   egg   gay   keg   cake   aim

may   make   came   game   gum   comb

no   know   name   neck

(*b*) ail   lay   laid   led   lake   delay

low   load   below   love   luck   lung

coal   goal   mail

(*c*) way   weigh   woe   web   wed   wedge

yoke   yellow

(*d*) 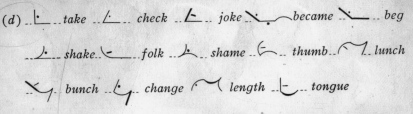 take — check — joke — became — beg

— shake — folk — shame — thumb — lunch

— bunch — change — length — tongue

In a phrase, the stroke *l* is used to represent the word *will*:

— *it will* — *which will* — *who will* — *they will*

— *it will be* — *it will have* — *they will be*

— *they will have*, etc.

EXERCISE 4

1. ....× 2. ....×

3. ....× 4. ....

....................? 5. ....?
.....×   ×

6. ....× 7. ....?
                                                                ×

EXERCISE 5

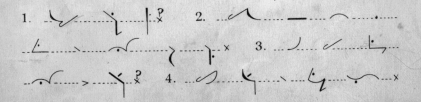

1. ....? 2. ....
.....×

..............................× 3. ....

.....................? 4. ....×
.....×

5.

6.

7.

8.

9.

EXERCISE 6

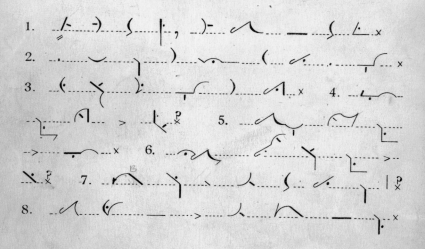

1.

2.

3.

4.

5.

6.

7.

8.

CHAPTER IV

11. First-Place Vowels

The next four vowels are written in the *first* place, that is, at the beginning of a stroke. When the *first* vowel in a word is a *first-place* vowel, the outline is written in *first* position, that is, the first downstroke or upstroke in the outline is written *above* the line. First position outlines consisting of horizontal strokes are written above the line.

(*a*) Long *ah* is represented by a heavy dot:

⸺ *pa*   ⸺ *ma*   ⸺ *calm*   ⸺ *palm*

(*b*) Short *ă* is represented by a light dot:

⸺ *at*   ⸺ *add*   ⸺ *path*   ⸺ *pal*   ⸺ *pack*   ⸺ *back*   ⸺ *bath*

⸺ *attack*   ⸺ *attach*   ⸺ *tank*   ⸺ *bank*   ⸺ *damage*   ⸺ *shadow*

⸺ *catch*   ⸺ *cash*   ⸺ *gang*   ⸺ *am*   ⸺ *among*   ⸺ *map*

⸺ *away*   ⸺ *lack*   ⸺ *manage*   ⸺ *annum*   ⸺ *package*

(*c*) Long *aw* is represented by a heavy dash:

⸺ *saw*   ⸺ *paw*   ⸺ *ball*   ⸺ *bought*   ⸺ *talk*   ⸺ *tall*

⸺ *auto*   ⸺ *chalk*   ⸺ *jaw*   ⸺ *law*

(*d*) Short *ŏ* is represented by a light dash:

⸺ *top*   ⸺ *odd*   ⸺ *doll*   ⸺ *dog*   ⸺ *job*   ⸺ *off*   ⸺ *shock*

⸺ *shop*   ⸺ *got*   ⸺ *lodge*   ⸺ *lock*   ⸺ *long*   ⸺ *knock*

⸺ *watch*   ⸺ *wash*

SHORT FORMS

____ *for*   *a* or *an*   *of*   *on*   *had* or *dollar*   *on the*

  but the (the signs for *on* and *but* slightly slanted)

EXERCISE 7

1.

2.

3.

4.

5.

6.

7.

8.

9.

10.

EXERCISE 8

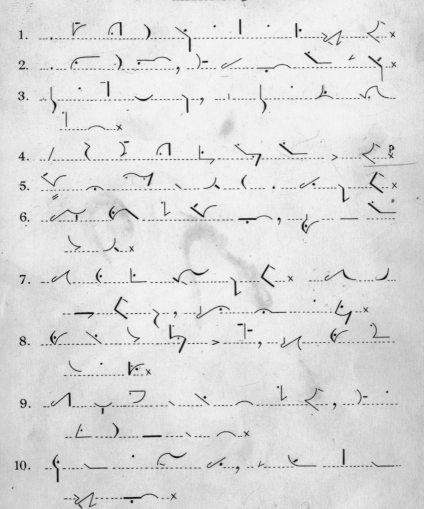

12. Second Position

When a *second-place* vowel is the *first* vowel in a word, the outline is written in *second* position, that is, the first downstroke or upstroke rests on the line:

⌐ *get*   *enough*   *Monday*   *engage*   *month*   *envelope*   *cup*   *leg*   *detail*   *coal*   *take*

EXERCISE 9

1.

2.

3.

4.

5.

6.

7.

8.

9.

10.

CHAPTER V

13. Third-Place Vowels

The last four vowels are written in the third place. When a third-place vowel comes between two strokes, it is put in third place before the second stroke.

When a third-place vowel is the first vowel in a word, the outline is written in third position, that is, the first downstroke or upstroke is written through the line.

(*a*) Long *ē* is represented by a heavy dot:

eat   tea   each   see   she   ease   fee

feed   deep   keep   leave   teach   theme

deal   meal   team

(*b*) Short *ĭ* is represented by a light dot:

if   bit   pick   big   ship   live   inch

kid   ill   bill   mill   milk   thick   width

(*c*) Long *ōō* is represented by a heavy dash:

chew   shoe   food   move   youth   tool

pool   cool   tooth

(*d*) Short *ŏŏ* is represented by a light dash:

book   took   look   wood   pull   push

baby   lucky   money   copy   many   lady

family   fifty   monthly   daily   appeal

Outlines consisting of horizontal strokes have no third position. Words like the following are written on the line:

_____ key _____ kick _____ cook _____ ink _____ King

Drop the ĭ vowel in the termination -ing:

_____ making _____ taking _____ leaving _____ living _____ looking

_____ asking _____ mailing _____ talking _____ washing

SHORT FORMS

_____ different or difference _____ wish _____ put _____ to be _____ owe

_____ can _____ go _____ ought _____ in or any

Short Form Derivatives: _____ being _____ doing _____ having _____ going

EXERCISE 10

1. _____

2. _____

3. _____

4. _____ 12×

5. _____

6. _____

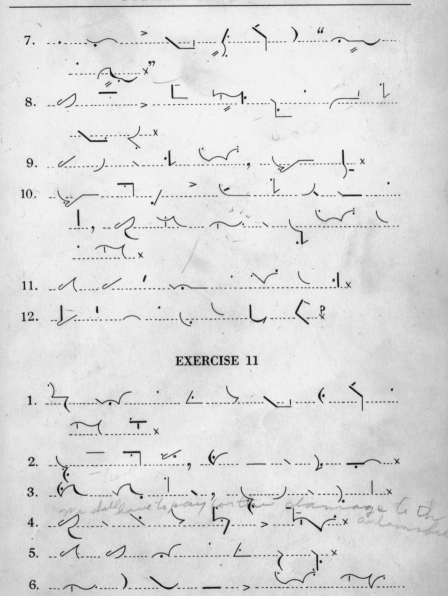

7.

8.

9.

10.

11.

12.

EXERCISE 11

1.

2.

3.

4.

5.

6.

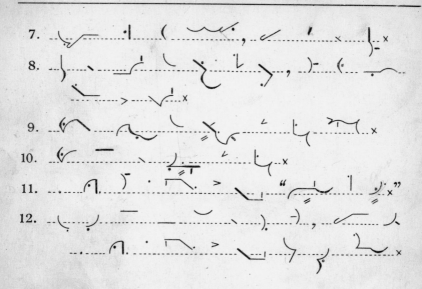

EXERCISE 12

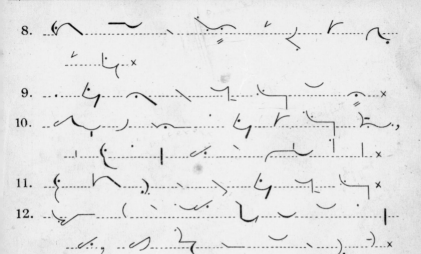

CHAPTER VI

14. Two Forms for *R*

Letter	Sign	Name	As in
R		ray	raw, reach, carry
		ar	car, air, dare

When *r* begins a word use ..../......:

....../... red .....\... raw ...\... road ....\.... rug .. \... rush .../.... ring

.../... reach ..\... ready .. \/.. readily ..\/.. retail \..... wrong

\..... railroad ...\/.. range \...... rank \...... relief \...... relieve

.../.. rich ..\..... reading

When a word begins with the combination *"vowel-r"* use ...\...:

..\.. air ...\.. arm ...\.. or ...\.. ear ..\/.. early ..\.. army

SHORT FORMS

..../... (~~up~~) are .../... (~~up~~) our or *hour* ...... (~~up~~) and .. /.. (~~up~~) *should*

NOTE: *Chay and Ray:* These strokes are somewhat similar, but they are different in slope and in the direction in which they are written. *Chay* is always written downward at a small angle from the vertical.

Ray is always written upward at a small angle from the horizontal.

EXERCISE 13

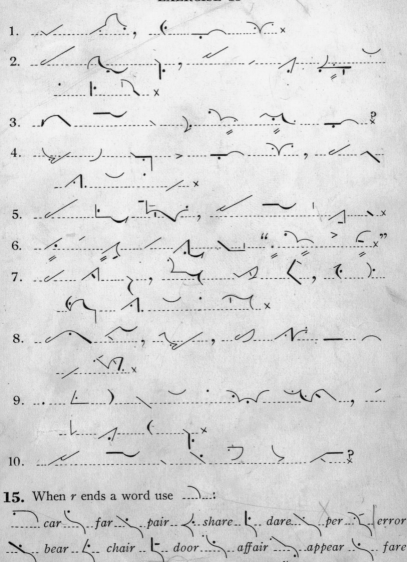

15. When *r* ends a word use ⌒:

car · far · pair · share · dare · per · error

bear · chair · door · affair · appear · fare

fear · four · fur · repair · assure

When a word ends with the combination *"r-vowel"* use ...../...:

.... *carry* .... *marry* .../... *ferry* .... *memory* .... *factory*

...../... *injury* .... *borrow* ...../... *dairy* .../... *jury* .... *narrow*

.../... *thorough* .../... *vary* .... *tomorrow*

SHORT FORMS

.... *your* .... *year* .)... *whose* .../... *large* .... *thank* or *thanked*

NOTE: In the phrase *"to go"* .... the vowel is inserted.

EXERCISE 14

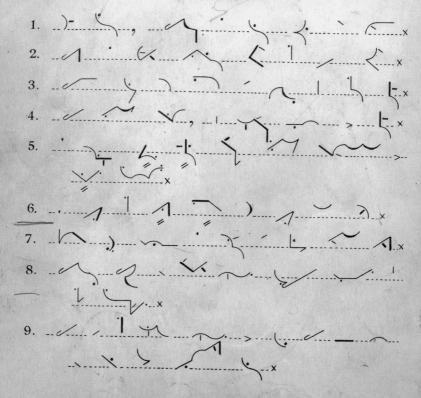

10.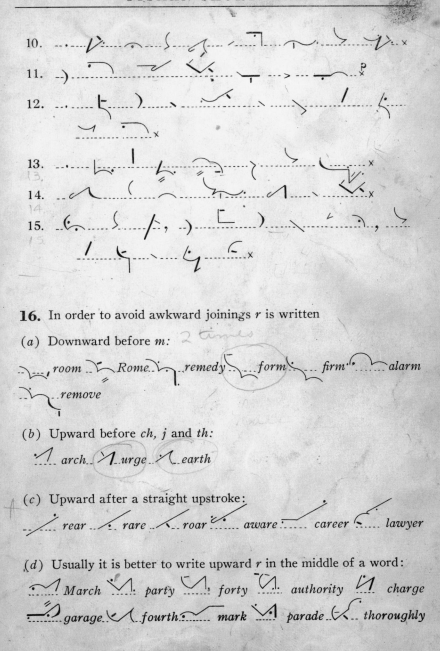

11.

12.

13.

14.

15.

16. In order to avoid awkward joinings *r* is written

(*a*) Downward before *m:*

room Rome. remedy form firm alarm remove

(*b*) Upward before *ch*, *j* and *th*:

arch urge earth

(*c*) Upward after a straight upstroke:

rear rare roar aware career lawyer

(*d*) Usually it is better to write upward *r* in the middle of a word:

March party forty authority charge garage fourth mark parade thoroughly

EXERCISE 15

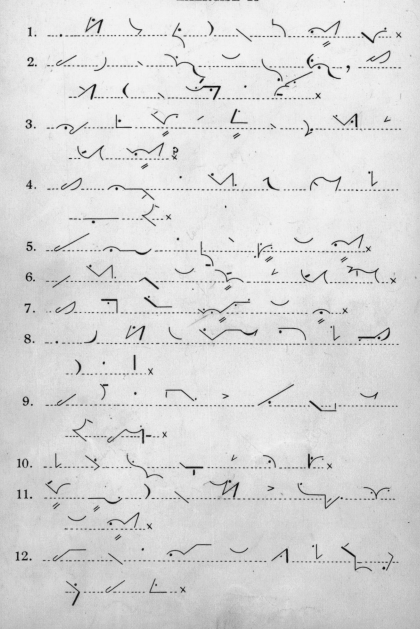

EXERCISE 16

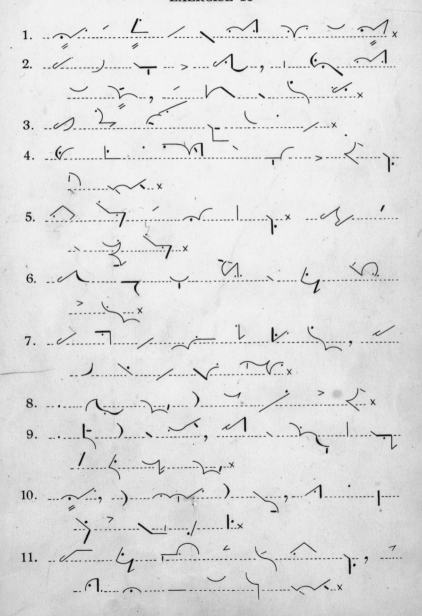

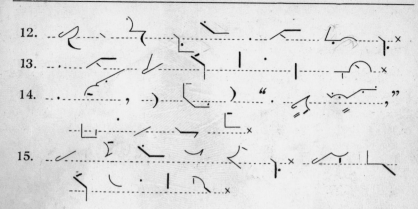

12.

13.

14.

15.

CHAPTER VII

17. Diphthongs

The four diphthongs (or double vowels) are *i, oi, ow,* and *u,* as heard in the words *I enjoy Gow's music.*

(*a*) The diphthong *i* is represented by a small angular mark written in the first vowel place:

pie   pipe   tie   type   die   by   buy

time   my   wide   lie   like   admire

alive   fire   five   tire   retire   arrive

pile   bite   dime   rye   knife   mile

china   shy   ripe

(*b*) The diphthong *oi* is represented by the same sign turned on its side. It is also written in the first vowel place:

boy   joy   enjoy   toy   boil   boiler

annoy   coil   toil   coy   alloy

(*c*) The diphthong *ow* is written as shown, in the third vowel place:

cow   out   loud   mouth   row   couch

outlay   lounge   county

(*d*) The diphthong *u* is represented by a small semicircle written in the third vowel place:

beauty   duty   failure   cure   endure   cube

bureau   tube   occupy

SHORT FORMS

...͌... I, eye, ...∧... how ...∟... why ...͡... beyond ...ი... you ...͡... with

...ͼ... when ...Ɔ... what ...ᴐ... would ...⌒... me

EXERCISE 17

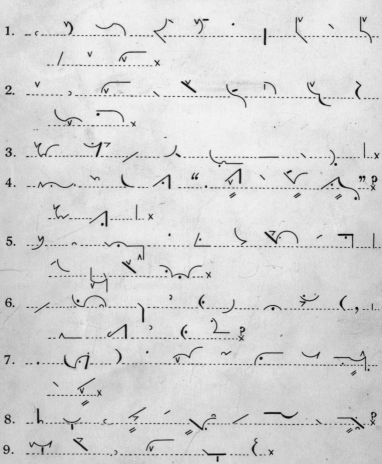

1.

2.

3.

4.

5.

6.

7.

8.

9.

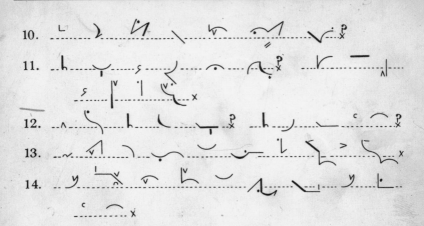

10.

11.

12.

13.

14.

EXERCISE 18

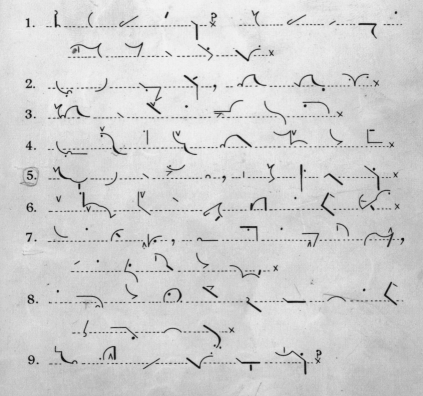

1.

2.

3.

4.

(5.)

6.

7.

8.

9.

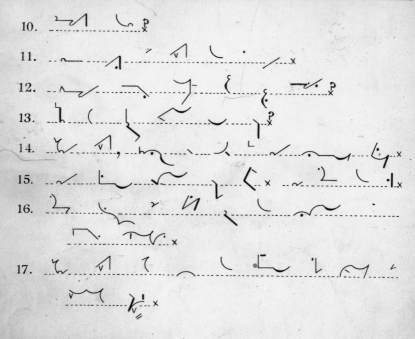

10.

11.

12.

13.

14.

15.

16.

17.

18. Joined Diphthongs

(*a*) The diphthong signs are joined to strokes when an easy joining can be made:

ice   eyes   item   idle   deny   oil   due

few   issue   new   avenue   review   value

renew   revenue   bough or *bow*.

(*b*) The sign for *ow* is contracted in the word   *now*.

(*c*) The sign for *i* is contracted before *l, m,* and *k,* to form the phrases

  I will (*I'll*)   I am (*I'm*)   I may   I can

(*d*) The short form *you* is turned on its side to form the phrases

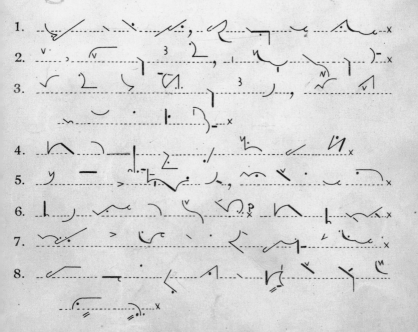

can you   give you   with you   when you   what you

would you   are you

19. Triphones

A small tick added to a diphthong sign indicates another vowel following the diphthong:

buying   dying   lying   via   Iowa   loyal

voyage   enjoying   power   shower   tower

towel   fewer   issuing

EXERCISE 19

1.

2.

3.

4.

5.

6.

7.

8.

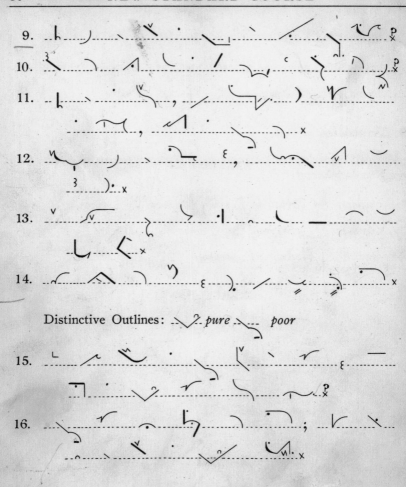

9.

10.

11.

12.

13.

14.

Distinctive Outlines: *pure* *poor*

15.

16.

EXERCISE 20

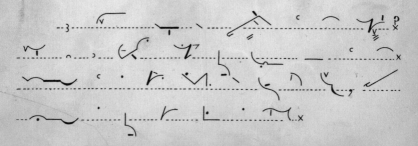

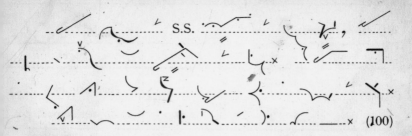

S.S.

(100)

EXERCISE 21

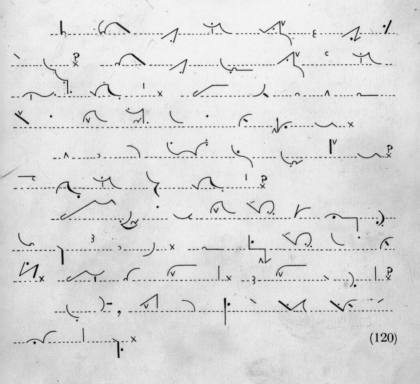

(120)

20. Consonant *H*

Letter	Sign	Name	As in
H		hay	he, high, hay
		hay	hope, happy, head

(*a*) When *h* is the only consonant stroke, or is followed by *k* or *g*, use the downward form:

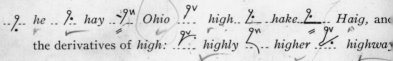

he　　hay　　Ohio　　high　　hake　　Haig, and

the derivatives of *high*: highly higher highway

(*b*) Use the upward form when *h* is joined to other consonants:

happy　hope　head　heavy　hotel　hang

huge　hurry

(*c*) The word *hope* is contracted to the stroke *p* to form the phrases:

I hope　I hope you will　I hope you are　we hope

we hope you will　we hope you are, etc.

(*d*) The word *he* is represented in the middle or at the end of a phrase by the short form . In other cases is used.

if he　　if he should, but　he will

EXERCISE 22

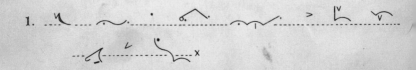

1.

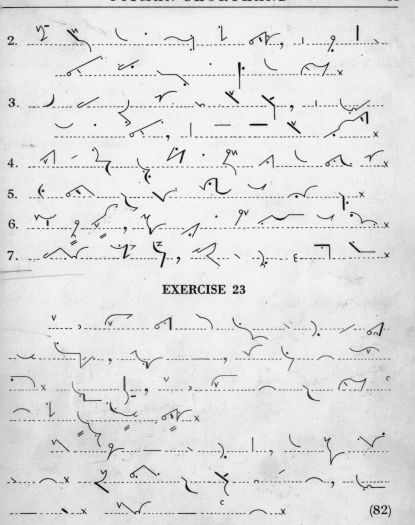

EXERCISE 23

(82)

CHAPTER VIII

21. S Circle

The very frequently occurring consonant *s,* and its corresponding heavy sound *z,* are represented by a small circle as well as by the stroke ..)..and ..)..

The small circle joins easily to other consonant strokes at the beginning, in the middle, or at the end of a word.

At the beginning of a word, the *s* circle is always read first; at the end of a word, the *s* circle is always read last.

The *s* circle is written inside a curve:

√ (a) face   these   shoes   loss   knows   name
   bills   else   anxious   less   months   leave
   shows   lose   miss   arms   ears   nice
   size   voice   invoice   announce   advice
   news   views   refuse   items   issues   errors
   forms   office   affairs

√ (b) safe   seem   slow   song   silk   sir
   small   Sunday   sense   sale   sales   save
   saving   sell   selling   sleep   snow   some
   soon   sun   since   similar   soil   south
   sign   salary

√ (c) message   absence   business   cousin   reason
   receive   receiving   passing   dozen   inside
   music   Wednesday

SHORT FORMS

... *has, or as* ...o.. *his, or is* ...ℓ... *several* ... *those* ..6.. *this*

..6.. *thus*

NOTE: ..ℓ.. *has the, or as the* ..℘.. *is the*

EXERCISE 24

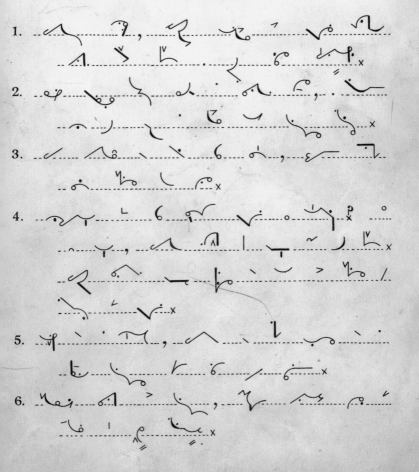

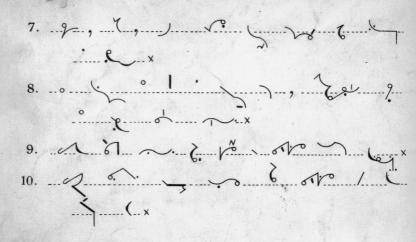

7.

8.

9.

10.

EXERCISE 25

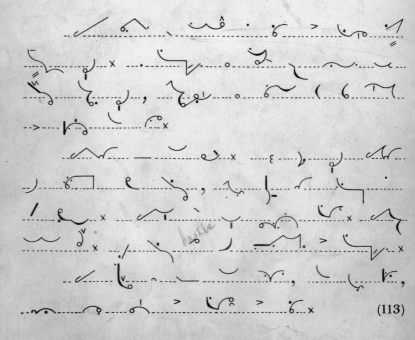

(113)

22. The *s* circle is written with a left motion to straight strokes.

(*a*) This means that it is written on the right side of straight down-strokes:

pass   days   copies   ladies   inches   piece

pages   choose

sat   said   sets   speech   such   sad

sit   city   cities   stay   spare   Saturday

side   suit   etc. (et cetera)   outside   decide

Tuesday

(*b*) It is written on the upper side of straight horizontal strokes and straight upstrokes:

guess   looks   box   fix   folks   case

cause   sick   soak   six   sake   secure

schedule   excuse   use   ways   yes   raise

house   carries   marries   varies   twice

sorry   series   service

SHORT FORMS

because   special, or *specially*   speak   subject, or *subjected*

The *s* circle is added to short forms:

speaks   subjects   yours   years   ours, or *hours*

wishes   thinks   thanks   goes   gives   comes

dollars   things   differences   puts, etc.

EXERCISE 26

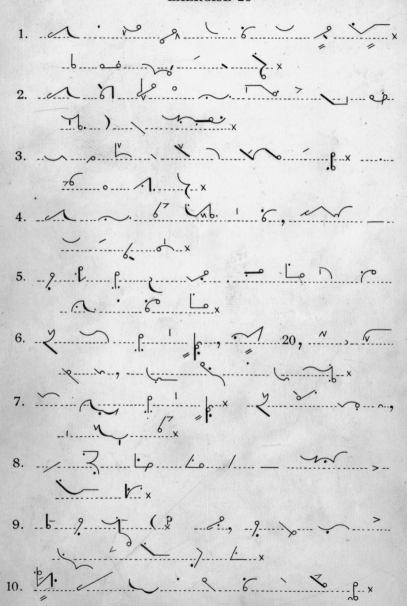

EXERCISE 27

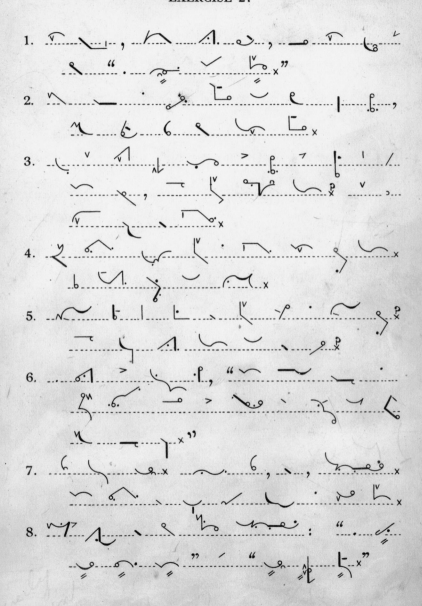

9.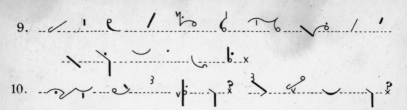

10.

23. Final *s* circle is used to represent the word *us* in the phrases

   for us   *to us*   *give us*   *take us*   *show us*

   making us   *charge us,* etc.

NOTE: *with us*   *when is*   *when is the*   *what is*

   what is the

EXERCISE 28

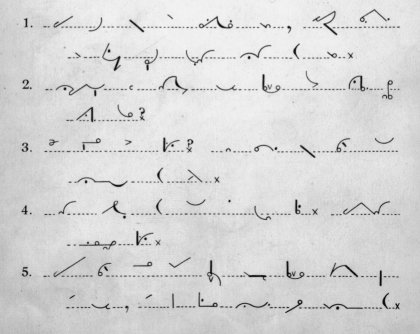

1.

2.

3.

4.

5.

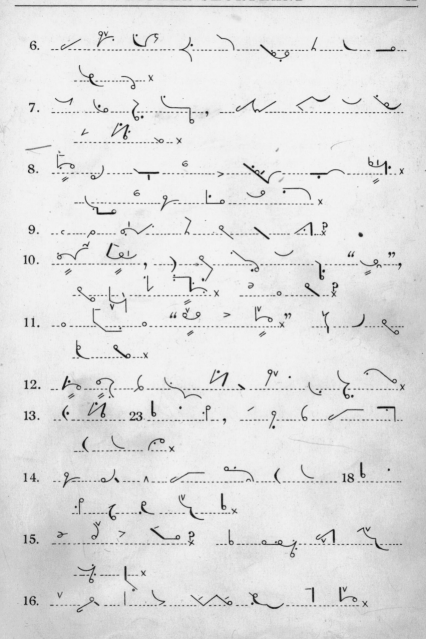

24. The *s* circle is written on the outside of the angle formed by two straight strokes:

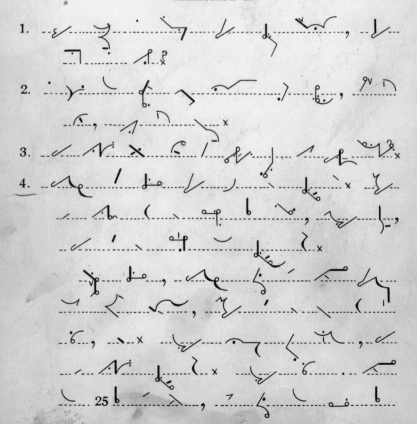

desk   discuss   dispose   besides   opposite   justice   sixty   succeed   receipt   history

25. The circle at the beginning of a word represents *s* only.

In the few words beginning with *z*, the stroke *z* is used:

zeal   zero   zenith

EXERCISE 29

1.

2.

3.

4.

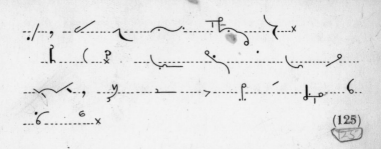

(125)

26. Although the words do not end with a vowel, upward *r* is used
following the curve and circle in words like

officer   answer   sincere

27. The stroke *l* may easily be written downward, and when it is attached
to the *s* circle it is written in the same direction as the circle:

vessel   nicely   cancel   council

lesson   listen   noiseless   muscle

EXERCISE 30

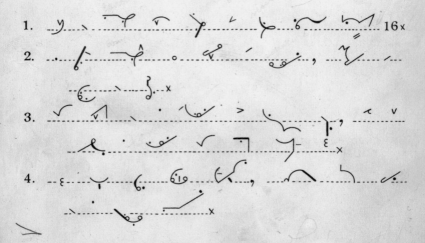

CHAPTER IX

28. *St Loop*

(*a*) A small loop, written in the same direction as the *s* circle, represents *st* (called "stee"):

   fast   *missed*   *must*   *honest*   *assist*   *list*   *invoiced*   *announced*

   stuff   *style*   *steel*   *still*   *stone*   *stem*   *store*

   post   *based*   *test*   *just*   *adjust*   *suggest*   *fixed*   *guest,* or *guessed*   *cost*   *waste*   *rest*   *haste*   *host*

   step   *state*   *stayed*   *stage*   *stock*   *story*

(*b*) The *st* loop represents either a light or heavy final sound:

   past   *paused*   *used*   *advised*   *refused*   *disposed*   *supposed*

Final *s* circle after a *st* loop is added as shown:

   lists   *posts*   *tests*   *wastes*   *adjusts*   *costs*   *suggests*

(*c*) The *st* loop may be written in the middle of a word:

   testing   *adjusting*   *suggesting*

SHORT FORMS

first   _most_   _influence_   _influenced_   _next_   _all_   _though_

NOTE: _although_   _all right_   _already_   _always_   _almost_   _also_   _as fast as_

EXERCISE 31

Distinctive Outlines: _cost_   _caused_

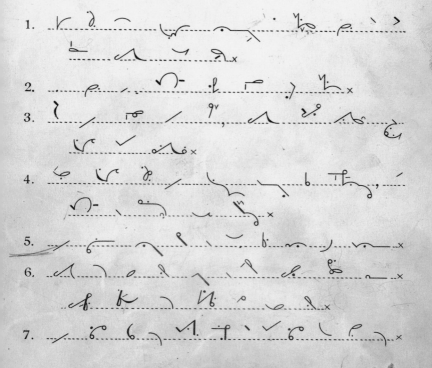

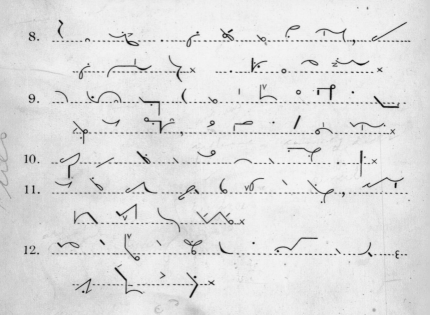

29. Str Loop

A large final loop, written in the same direction as the *s* circle, represents *ster:*

master   register   semester   poster   minister
administer   investor   Hester   Chester   Rochester
coaster   roadster

The *ster* loop is not used at the beginning of a word.

The *s* circle is added as shown: masters   registers   posters
investors

EXERCISE 32

1.

2.

3.

4.

5.

6.

7.

8.

9.

10.

30. *Ses Circle*

(*a*) A large final circle represents *ses*, or *sez*. This large circle is written in the same direction as the circle *s*:

faces   *losses*   *services*   *cases*   *pieces*

boxes   *taxes*   *success*   *passes*   *fixes*

causes   *uses*   *chooses*   *supposes*

(*b*) The large circle also represents *ses* in the middle of a word:

necessary   *necessity*   *successive*   *successfully*

(*c*) Any vowel other than short *ĕ* between the two *s's* is indicated by writing the vowel sign inside the circle:

basis   *insist*   *exhaust*   *resist*   *census*   *Texas*

Kansas   *Mississippi*   *exercise*   *exercises*

SHORT FORMS

themselves   *ourselves*   *as is*   *is as*   *myself*

himself   *itself*   *much*

EXERCISE 33

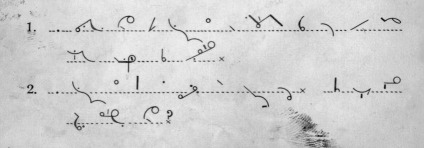

1.

2.

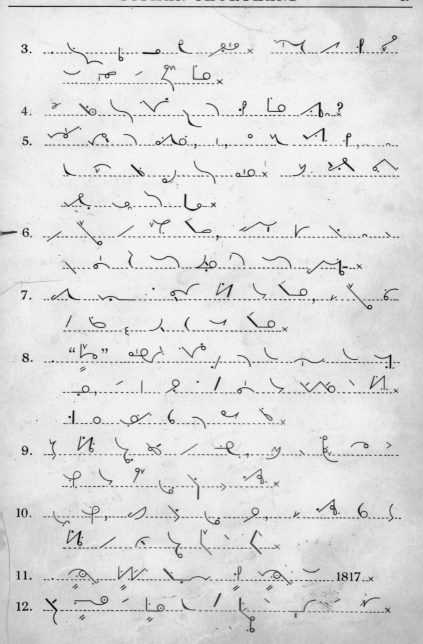

EXERCISE 34

(Write in Shorthand)

(Phrases are indicated by hyphens. Short Forms are indicated by italic type.)

1. *Are-you* enjoying *your* study *of-this subject? I-*hope-*you-are.*

2. *When you-can* write these exercises fast, *you-*will-*be on-your* way *to-*making *your* living *in a* business office.

3. *But* outside *of-its* value *to-you, I-*hope-*you* like-*the subject for-itself.*

4. *As you* know, *this subject is* widely used *in* business offices, *but it-has* many uses besides *this.*

5. *You-can* use *it for-*many *different* purposes. *Can-you* name some *of-them?*

6. *The* success *of-*many *a* famous head *of a large* business firm *is* due *to-his* study *of-this subject. It-was-the first* step *in-his* business career.

7. Write-*the* signs *as-fast-as you-can. Al*ways read back *what you-*write.

8. Each time *you-*write *an* exercise *you-should* write *it* faster *and* read *it* back faster.

9. Write-*the* forms just-*as they* appear *in-this* text.

10. *In-*time *you-may,* if-*you wish,* write these same forms *as-fast-as you-can speak.*

31. *Sw* Circle

(a) A large initial circle represents *sw* (called "sway"). The *sw* circle is written in the same direction as the *s* circle:

sweep *sweet* *sweetest* *swell* *swelling*

swim *swing* *swear* *switch* *swiftest*

swayed

(*b*) The *sw* circle is used to represent the words *as we* in the phrases

ℛ... *as we have* ℛ... *as we think* ...🌙.. *as we shall* ..🌙.. *as we wish*

◯... *as we may* ℒ... *as we know* ℒ... *as we can* ℒ... *as we are,* etc.

It is also used to form the phrase ◯... *as well as.*

(*c*) The large circle is used to represent the two *s*'s in the phrases

..6.. *this is* ..6.. *this is the* ..6.. *this city* ℒℒ... *as soon as*

ℒℒ... *as soon as possible*

SHORT FORMS

..🌙.. *United States* ..🌙... *United States of America* ..✓.. *New York*

..ℓ.. *largest*

EXERCISE 35

1.

2.

3.

4.

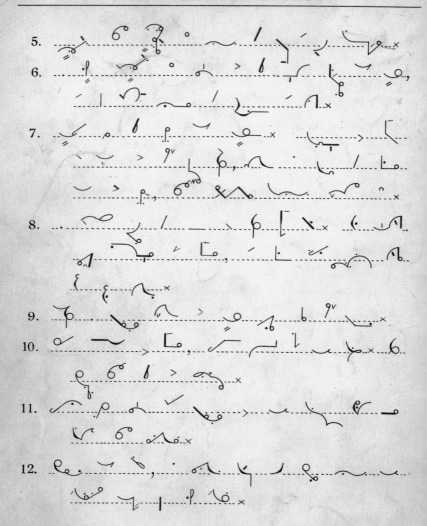

32. Vowel Indication

(*a*) A circle or loop is always read first at the beginning of a word. If a vowel begins a word, we must write a stroke in order to place the initial vowel sign:

sack but *ask* *sleep* but *asleep* *sum* but *assume* *scope* but *escape* *side* but *aside*

(*b*) A circle or loop is always read last at the end of a word. If a word ends in a vowel, we must write a stroke in order to place the final vowel sign:

bees but *busy* *police* but *policy* *honest* but *honesty* *lace* but *lazy* *modest* but *modesty*

(*c*) If a vowel occurs between *s* and *t,* the *st* loop is not used:

deposed but *deposit* *vast* but *visit* *opposed* but *opposite* *best* but *beset* *rest* but *recite*

The outline thus indicates the presence or absence of a vowel sound.

(*d*) As there are no places alongside a circle or loop for placing vowel signs, we must write

us *so* *say* *says* *see* *sees, seas, seize,* or *cease* *seized* or *ceased* *seizes* or *ceases* *ice* *essay* *eyes* *ease* *easy* *owes*

Special phrases: *so much* *too much* *how much* *as much as* *inasmuch as* *as much as possible* *as early as possible* *as far as possible*

SHORT FORMS

⤴ *especial* or *especially*   ⌣ *language* or *owing*   *young*

anything   *nothing*   *something*

NOTE: In Pitman Shorthand we represent all the consonants we hear in the words we write. Except for the "short forms", where for the sake of extreme brevity we use only one or two of the consonants in a word, we do not resort to the expedient of writing only some part of a word. This is one of the reasons for the remarkable legibility of Pitman Shorthand.

As we proceed we will find that the various abbreviating devices of the system enable us to represent all the consonants in words in concise, legible, and rapid shorthand forms. These outlines are so clearly distinctive that it is unnecessary to insert the vowel signs. The outlines are perfectly legible without them.

In addition to writing a full outline of the consonants, we employ a means of indicating the presence or absence of a vowel with practically every abbreviating device of the system, and also we have position writing, which is an expedient highly prized by the fastest and most accurate shorthand writers in the world. It is not surprising, therefore, that the system is so legible.

From now on, we will omit the vowel signs in the sentences and letters, and we will speed on our way writing the outlines just as they appear in the text. You will note that we insert a vowel sign occasionally, to eliminate any possibility of hesitation in reading back your notes.

EXERCISE 36

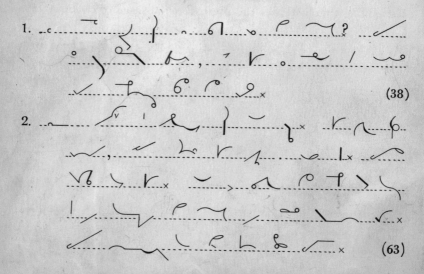

1.   (38)

2.   (63)

EXERCISE 37

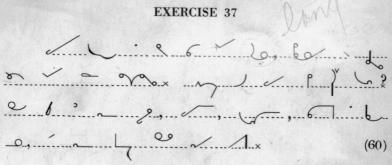

(60)

EXERCISE 38

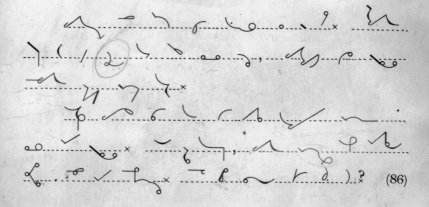

(86)

EXERCISE 39

1.

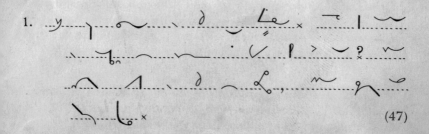

(47)

2.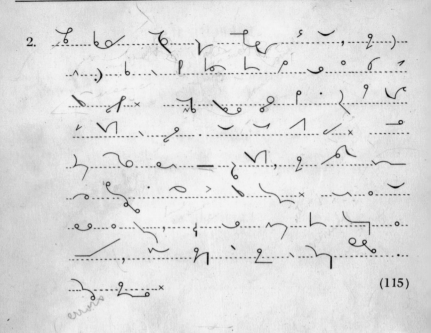

(115)

EXERCISE 40

(*Write in Shorthand*)

1. Suppose some big customer *of-yours* ceased *to*-deal-*with-you*. *What-would you do?* *We-think-you would* write *to-him*, asking if-*he had any special* reason *for-his* silence.

2. *This-is what we-are*-now asking-*you*. *Although in-the* past *our* business *with-you in-this*-city *was* extensive, *several* months *have* elapsed since *you* last *had any* dealings *with-us*. *We would* like *to* know *why*, *as-we-are* unaware *of any* failure *to-give-you-the* best service.

3. *We-are* always desirous *of*-satisfying *all-our* customers, *large* buyers or small. *We* assure-*you we-shall-do* anything *we-can to put things* right, if-*you think our* service *in-any*-way faulty. (119)

EXERCISE 41

(Write in Shorthand)

1. *I-have*-seen *your* notice *in to*day's "Star", *and-I should*-like *to-have* details *of-your* new Masters' Reading Series. *I-think* such *a* series *should* make *a* wide appeal, *and-I-wish-you much* success *with-it.*

2. Many *of-those who have*-seen my set *of* "Stories *of-the* Earth, Sea, *and* Sky" *speak* highly *of-it, and-several, I*-know, *have* bought similar sets *for-themselves.*

3. *I*-am-sorry *you have* allowed "Poster Designing" *to*-go out *of* stock. Such *a* book, *it*-seems *to-me, should-have a large* sale, *as* so-many *are*-now taking-up-*the* study *of-this-subject. In*-view *of-this,* may *I* suggest *a* new issue? (116)

CHAPTER X

33. Halving

Strokes are halved to indicate a following *t* or *d*.

(*a*) In words of one syllable a light stroke is halved to indicate a following *t*:

. . . *not* . . . *note* . . . *aunt* . . . *act* . . . *caught* . . . *coat*

. . . *cut* . . . *met* . . . *meet* . . . *fat* . . . *fight* . . . *thought*

. . . *art* . . . *wait* . . . *yet* . . . *lot* . . . *light* . . . *slight*

. . . *late* . . . *let* . . . *stopped* . . . *asked* . . . *talked* . . . *kept*

. . . *reached* . . . *shipped* . . . *marked* . . . *left* . . . *checked*

NOTE: . . . *night*

The *s* circle is always read last: . . . *notes* . . . *acts* . . . *thoughts*

. . . *lots* . . . *waits* . . . *nights*

(*b*) In words of one syllable a heavy stroke is halved to indicate a following *d*:

. . . *bad* . . . *bed* . . . *died* . . . *dead* . . . *God* . . . *good*

. . . *loved* . . . *charged* . . . *lived* . . . *changed*

SHORT FORMS

. . . *quite* . . . *could* . . . *that* . . . *without* . . . *sent* . . . *wished*

EXERCISE 42

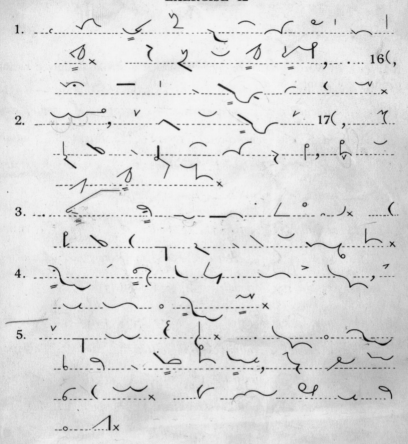

EXERCISE 43

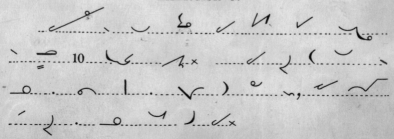

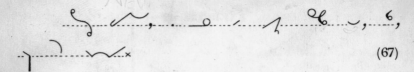

(67)

34. (*a*) In words of two or more syllables, a stroke is halved to indicate a following *t* or *d*:

(1) attached · answered · except · suggested · avoid · market · recent · absent · admit · arrived · engaged · enjoyed · estate · stated · exact · result · benefit · booklet

(2) actually · writing · badly · lately · entire · entirely · evidence · sometimes · waiting · certain · goodbye · absolutely

(3) omit · omitted · note · noted · accept · accepted · submit · submitted · await · awaited · limit · limited · visit · visited · list · listed · remit · remitted · deduct · deducted · notify · notified · invited

(*b*) A half length stroke is not written through the line to indicate a third position. Words like the following are written on the line:

east · feet · fit · sheets · bid · did · written · invite · indeed · needed · instead · little · moved · Pittsburgh

(c) Where a final diphthong is joined, a stroke is halved fo indicate a final t or d:

‑ᴋ‑ doubt ‑‑‑ about ‑ᴍ‑ bowed ‑‑ᴄ‑cute ‑‑ʃ‑ issued

EXERCISE 44

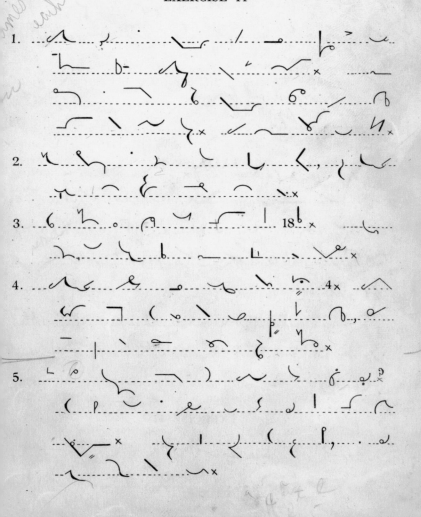

EXERCISE 45

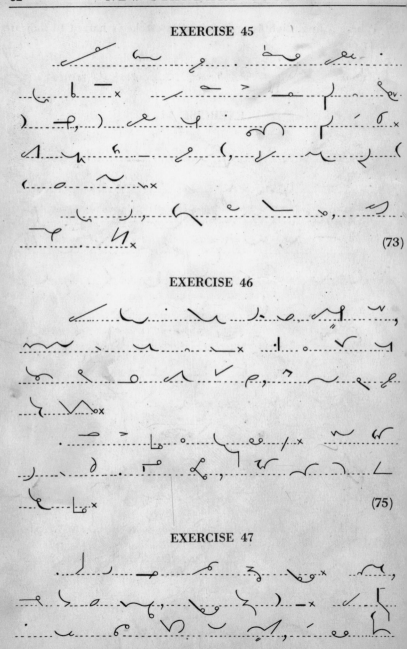

(73)

EXERCISE 46

(75)

EXERCISE 47

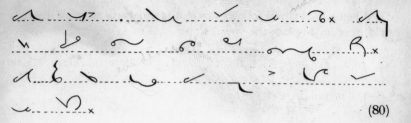

(80)

EXERCISE 48
(*Write in Shorthand*)

1. Little by little *all of*-us form habits. Sometimes *we* form good habits, *and*-sometimes *our* habits *are* bad. *It-is* certain *that-the* habit *of* accuracy *is* likely *to-be·of-the-most* value *to*-us *in a* business office. (41)

2. *We-have-sent several* notes *to-you* asking-*you* to pay-*the* bill *for-the*-goods *you* bought six-months-ago, *but-you have*-not answered *any of-them.*

   We-are-sorry *to* say *that* now *we-shall-have* to-take-*the usual* steps *to*-avoid-*the* loss *of-our* money, *if-your* check *is*-not received by-*the first of next* month. *We* urge *you* to-mail *your* check *to*-us *without*-delay. (74)

35. (*a*) To avoid confusion with ⌐ *should* and ⌐ *and,* we do not

   use ⌐ *rt* and ⌐ *rts* standing alone. Therefore we write

   ⌐ *rate* ⌐ *rates* ⌐ *right* ⌐ *rights* ⌐ *write* ⌐ *wrote*

   ⌐ *route*

(*b*) In certain words, where the proper length of a halved stroke would not clearly show, the halving principle is not employed:

   ⌐ *fact* ⌐ *effect* ⌐ *liked* ⌐ *locate* ⌐ *minute*

   ⌐ *select* ⌐ *territory* ⌐ *tonight*

(c) When a final vowel follows *t* or *d*, it is necessary to write the stroke
t or *d* in order to place the vowel sign:

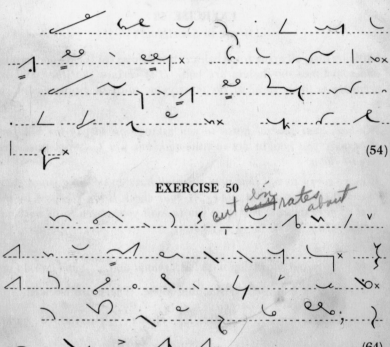

pity   *body*   *forty*   *window*   *empty*   *into*

Cincinnati

EXERCISE 49

(54)

EXERCISE 50

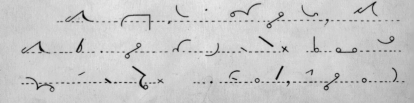

(64)

EXERCISE 51

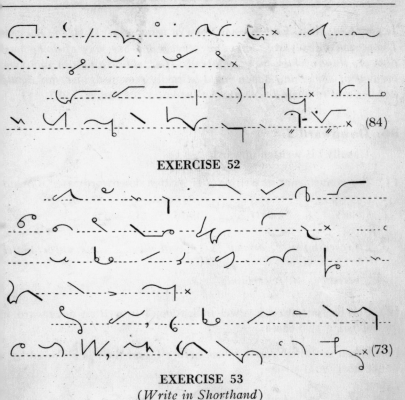

EXERCISE 52

EXERCISE 53
(*Write in Shorthand*)

Do-you know *that-we* sell good tires? *It-is*-not-necessary *for-you* to buy tires now *in a* repair shop, *for our* store now carries *them*. *You-can* buy *them when you-are in-the* store, just-*as you would* select silks, or *something for-your* house.

These tires *are* good value, *and*-they sell rapidly. Each *of-them* carries *our* guarantee. (64)

EXERCISE 54
(*Write in Shorthand*)

It-is quite some time since *you* bought *anything in-this* store. *I-am*-writing *to-you myself, because I should-be* sorry *to*-lose *your* custom.

It-may-*be that*-*we*-*have* offended *you in*-some-way. If-*this*-*is*-*the* case
I-hope-*you*-will write *to*-*me*. *Our* service *and our* way *of*-*do*ing business *are things which*-*we* boast about. *It*-*would*-*be* a pity *to* stay awa
because *of*-something *which could*-*be* easily remedied, *and you*-*should*
not hesitate *to*-write *to*-*me and* let-*me*-know-*the* cause. (95)

36. Downward L

Usually *l* is written upward.

(1) For convenience in writing, *l* is written downward after *n* or *ng*

..¥.. *only* ..6.. *unless* ..¥.. *until* ......(*canal* ..6. *analysi*

..¿.*exceedingly*..¥..*annual*..↘..*evidently* ..↗.*unfortunatel*

..¥. *recently*..∿..*certainly*

(2) For the purpose of vowel indication, *l* is written downward in
the following two cases.

(*a*) When an initial vowel comes before *l*, and the *l* is followed by a
simple horizontal stroke:

..C.. *alone* ..C.. *along*..C..*Ellen* ..C. *alike* ..C.*elm*..C...*Illinois*

..C..*Elmira* ..C.. *elect* ..C..*elected* but ..⌢.. *long* ..v.. *like*

..⌒.. *Lena* ..⌒..*lake* ..v.. *lime*

(*b*) When *l* follows *f, v, sk,* or a straight upstroke, and a vowel does
not end the word:

..¿.. *fail* ..¿. *fall* ..¿. *awful* ..\. *feel* ..\. *feeling* ..¿. *fell*

..¿. *fill* ..¿. *full* ..\. *veal* ..⌐. *skill* ..⟋. *rule* ..⌐. *scale*

..\. *barrel* ..↘.*successful* ..∧. *useful* ..∧. *Yale* ..∧ *rail*

When a vowel ends the word, *l* is written upward:

..... folly ..... awfully ..... fellow ..... fully ..... lovely

..... successfully ..... usefully ..... yellow ..... rely ..... sickly

NOTE. Special Outlines: ..... *volume* ..... *column* ..... *film*

SHORT FORMS

..... inform-ed ..... never, November ..... satisfactory ..... respect-ed

..... expect-ed ..... inspect-ed-ion ..... January ..... February

..... together ..... altogether ..... insurance

EXERCISE 55

1.

2.

3.

4.

5.

6.

7.

8.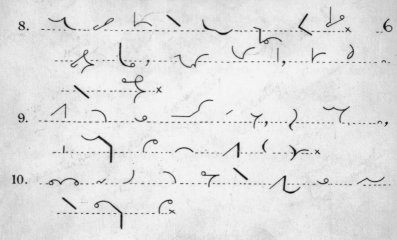

9.

10.

EXERCISE 56

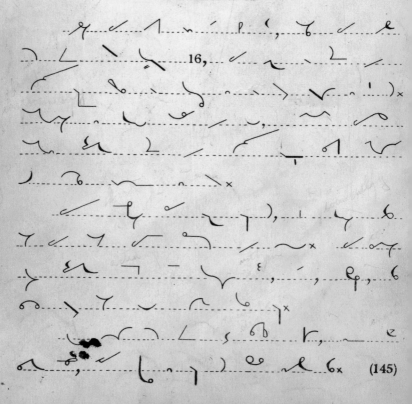

(145)

EXERCISE 57

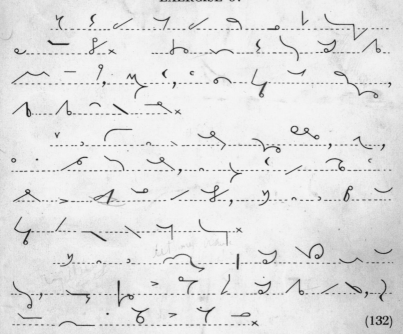

(132)

37. Abbreviated *W*

A small initial semicircle, written as shown, is used as an abbreviation for *w* at the beginning of *k, g, m,* and upward and downward *r:*

week or weak ___ walk ___ walked ___ wig ___ womanly

___ worry ___ worth ___ worthy ___ were ___ wear ___ wire

___ work ___ worked ___ worse ___ worst

NOTE: The small semicircle is always read first. When a vowel begins a word, the stroke *w* must be written:

___ awake ___ awoke ___ aware

Special Phrases: ___ you were ___ which were ___ who were

___ they were ___ we were

EXERCISE 58

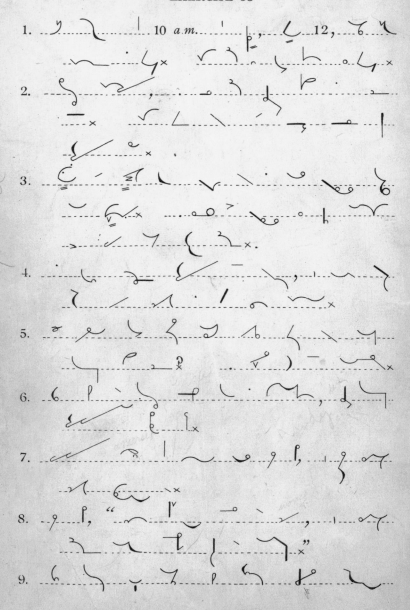

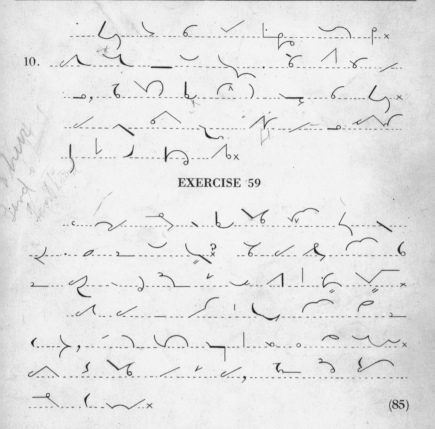

EXERCISE 59

(85)

EXERCISE 60
(Write in Shorthand)

I-wish to-thank-you for-the catalog *which-you-*were good-enough *to-*mail *to-me* recently. *Several* books listed *on* page 21 appear *to-be* just *what I-*am looking *for. I-have* marked *them on-the* attached sheet.

*Although I-think that-*these books *should-be* useful *to-me in-*my work, *I would* like *to inspect them to* see if-*they would-be satisfactory. Can any of-the* books *be sent* back *to-you* if, *when I-have* looked at-*them, I-*decide *that-*they *would-*not-*be satisfactory for-*my purpose? (96)

CHAPTER XI

38. Double Consonants — *Pl Series*

A small beginning hook, written on the circle side of straight downstrokes and *k* and *g,* forms a series of double consonants:

pl   *bl*   *tl*   *dl*   *chl*   *jl*   *kl*   *gl*

These double consonants are called *pel, bel,* etc. They are pronounced as a single sound (pl-a, play), and the vowel signs are placed to them just as they are placed to single consonants.

play   place   places   placing   placed

replace   plate   played   plus   blue   black

blame   blank   block   class   clear   clerk

close   closed   enclose   cloth   clothes   club

claim   glass   glad

apply   applied   replied   simple   couple   able

enable   double   table   reasonable   terrible

oblige   total   entitled   include   included

including   local   uncle   article   single

duplicate   o'clock

Distinctive Forms: valuable   available

An *s* circle at the beginning is written inside the hook of the *pl* series:

supply   supplied   split   settle   settled

possible   possibly   displace   disclose   physical

exclusive

SHORT FORMS

people — belief, believe, or *believed* — tell — till

deliver, delivered, or *delivery* — call — called — equal,

equally — equaled, or *cold* — building, or *able-to*

Phrases: — at all — by all — I believe

EXERCISE 61

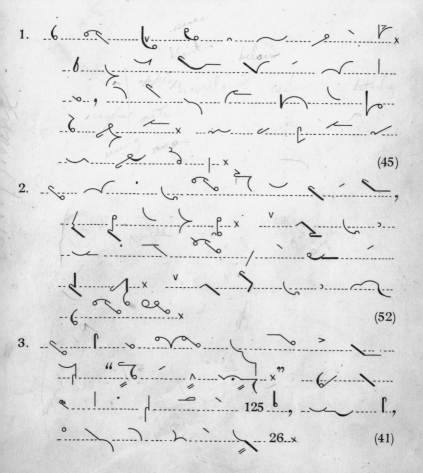

1. (45)

2. (52)

3. 125 26 (41)

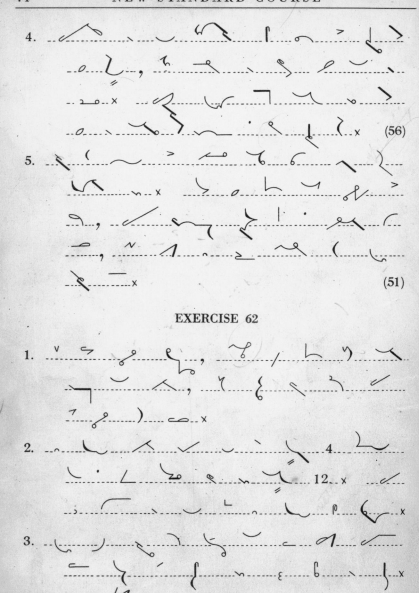

4. .... (56)

5. .... (51)

EXERCISE 62

1. ....

2. ....

3. .... (46)

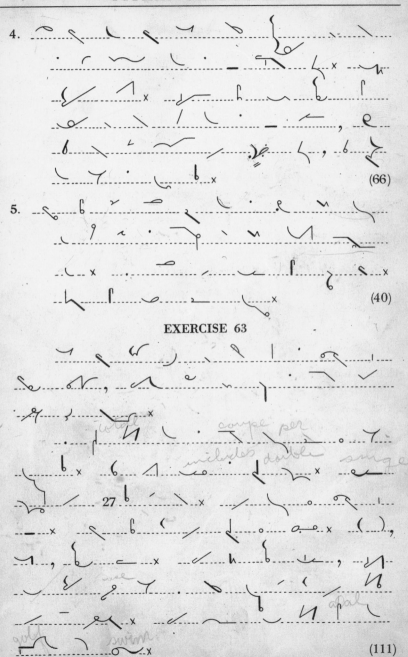

4.

(66)

5.

(40)

EXERCISE 63

(111)

EXERCISE 64

(Write in Shorthand)

We-enclose *a* booklet *which gives* details *of-our* plate-glass window *insurance*. *When-you* renew *your insurance we-believe it*-will pay *you to*-take-out *this* type *of* policy.

You-will-note *that-we-are able-to give-you especially* useful service. *As*-soon-*as-we* receive *your* claim *we* replace-*the* glass. *Your* claim *is* settled *without*-delay, *and a* check *large* enough *to* pay *for all-the* damage, including *any* damage *to-your* window display, *is sent to-you*.

If-*you wish, we-shall-be-glad to-have* somebody *call on-you to-tell-you anything you*-may *wish to* know about *this insurance*. (108)

39. Double Consonants — *Pr Series*

A small initial hook, written on the non-circle side of straight downstrokes and *k* and *g,* forms a series of double consonants:

   pr   *br*   *tr*   *dr*   *chr*   *jr*   *kr*   *gr*

These double consonants are called *per, ber,* etc.

(a)   *pray*   *press*   *price*   *propose*   *presume*

  present   *April*   *break*   *branch*   *bridge*

  bring   *bright*   *broke*   *brought*   *try*

  trial   *trip*   *truly*   *trust*   *trusting*   *dry*

  drop   *dream*   *dress*   *address*   *grow*

  group   *greatest*   *grades*   *across*   *crop*

  cream   *cry*   *credit*   *crowd*

(b) ⁓ better ⁓ labor ⁓ teacher ⁓ manager ⁓ proceed

⁓ progress ⁓ properly ⁓ increased ⁓ program

⁓ problem ⁓ proud ⁓ degree ⁓ agreed ⁓ daughter

⁓ water ⁓ withdraw ⁓ practical ⁓ liberal ⁓ graduate

⁓ October

SHORT FORMS

⁓ Dr., doctor ⁓ dear ⁓ during ⁓ truth ⁓ principal,

principally, or *principle* ⁓ liberty ⁓ member, remember, or

remembered ⁓ number, or *numbered* ⁓ care

EXERCISE 65

1. [shorthand outlines]

2. [shorthand outlines] 87⁵⁰ [shorthand outlines] 463 [shorthand outlines] 16 [shorthand outlines] 85⁵⁰ [shorthand outlines] (65)

3. [shorthand outlines] 16 [shorthand outlines] 463 [shorthand outlines] (42).

4.

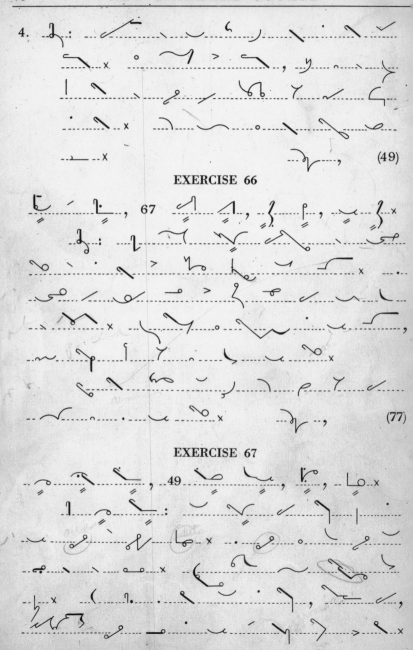

(49)

EXERCISE 66

67

(77)

EXERCISE 67

, 49

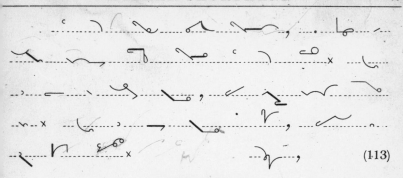

(113)

EXERCISE 68
(*Write in Shorthand*)

Dr. Thomas Waters, 21 Bridge Avenue, Cincinnati, Ohio

Dear Dr. Waters: *We-are* taking-*the liberty of* asking-*you to* address *our* graduates at *our* exercises *on January* 29. *Our principal and* teachers, *as*-well-*as-the* graduates, *would-be* proud *to-have-you deliver an* address. *As-the principal* speaker *on-our* program *we*-know-*that what-you-would tell-us would-be* remembered by-*all our* graduates *for*-many-*years to-come*.

We-know-*that-you have* many *calls to-speak, and-that your* time *is* exceedingly valuable, *but-we*-feel *that-you*-will-*be*-glad *to*-talk *to-us if-you* possibly *can*. *We*-trust *that-you*-will-*be*-able-*to* accept. *Yours*-truly,

(109)

40. (*a*) When an initial circle or loop is written on the same side as the hook of the *pr* series, the *r* is included:

spring   strange   strong   street   straight

strength   supper   separate   secretary   sweeter

sticker

(*b*) Both hook and circle are shown in the middle of a word:

extra   extremely   express

(*c*) When *skr* or *sgr* follows *t* or *d*, the combinations are written thus.

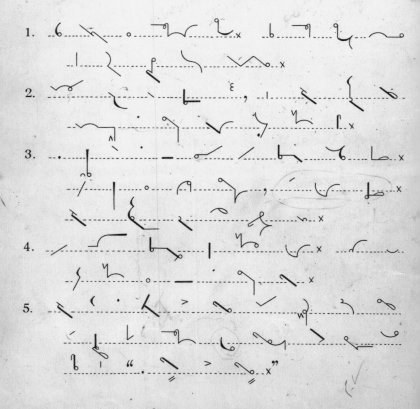

       describe   *disgrace*   *disagree*

Distinctive Forms: *propriety*   *property*

                propose   *purpose*

SHORT FORMS

    description   *surprise*   *surprised*

EXERCISE 69

1.

2.

3.

4.

5.

EXERCISE 70

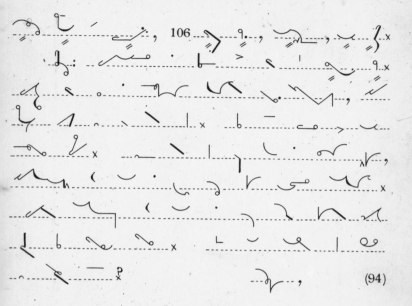

106 .....

(94)

41. Special Use of Double Consonants

In a special group of words, the double consonant strokes are used although a distinct vowel comes between a consonant and *l* or *r*. The double consonant strokes are employed in order to secure briefer or more facile outlines. The most important of these words are given below.

Although it is seldom necessary to vocalize these special outlines, a dot vowel may be indicated by writing a small circle instead of the dot, either after, or before the double consonant stroke:

parcel *darling* *dark* *charm* *direct* *directly*

The short *ĕ* vowel is never indicated in words like *person* *girl* *term*

A dash vowel, or a diphthong, is shown by writing the vowel sign c
diphthong sign through, or at the beginning, or at the end of the stroke

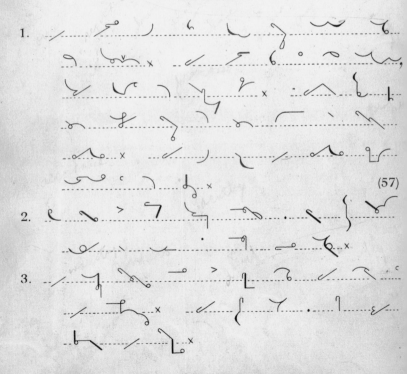

college *accordance* *accordingly* *course* *cou*

church *occurred* *record* *purchase* *corre*

collect *courtesy* *attorney* *lecture* *literatu*

lectures

Distinctive Forms: *regard* *regret*

EXERCISE 71

1.

(57)

2.

3.

4.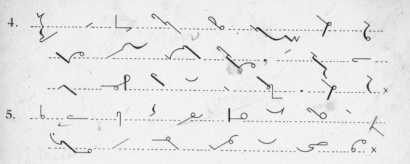

5.

EXERCISE 72

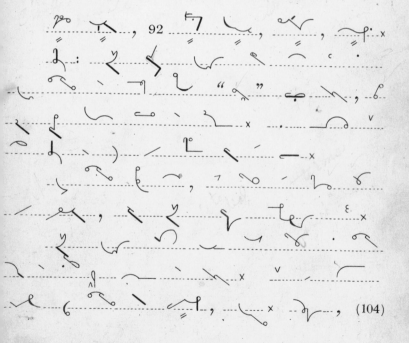

EXERCISE 73

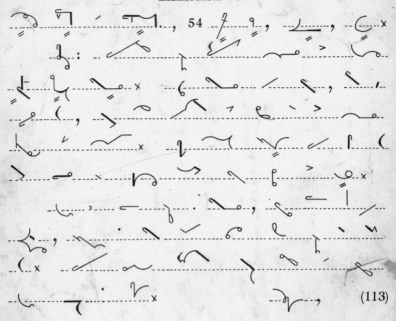

(113)

EXERCISE 74

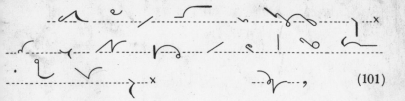

(101)

EXERCISE 75
(Write in Shorthand)

1. If-*you*-will bring *me a* supply *of*-samples *of-this* new breakfast food, *I*-will-try *to*-close-*the* deal *with-the* firm *myself.*

2. *During-the* course *of*-my lecture, *I-shall* try *to* show *how-the* progress *of* art *is* related *to-the* growth *of* industry.

3. *When I*-know *what-the* proposed water power scheme includes, *I*-shall-be-glad *to*-express my views.

4. *A* loud voice troubles *and* annoys us. Pleasant voices resemble sweet music.

5. Castles *in-the* air *are* fabrics *which* soon crumble, *but* dreamers *have* solved many *a* pressing problem.

6. Few *people are* able *themselves to* better-*the* labor *of-those* they blame.

EXERCISE 76
(Write in Shorthand)

Peter Semple *and*-Sons, 92 Court Street, Rochester, New-York.

Dear-Sirs: Due *to-the* rapidly increasing cost *of* copper *and* steel, *we-are*-obliged *to* increase-*the* prices *of*-many *of-the* articles included *in* our catalog. *We* extremely regret-*the* necessity *of* passing *on-the* higher charges *to-our* customers, *but* at-*the* present-time *this-is-the* only possible course *we-can* follow.

You-will-*be* notified *when* better terms *are* available *on-our* supplies, *and-we-are* thus enabled *to*-reduce-*the* prices. *Yours*-truly, (79)

42. Double Consonants — *Curves*

(*a*) A small initial hook, written on the inside of curves, forms a series of double consonant strokes, *fr, vr,* etc.

Friday   afraid   average   every   everybody

other   otherwise   author   shrub   shrink

dinner   pressure   measure   leisure   enclosure

favor   favorable   favored   endeavor   honor

manner   effort   efforts   sooner   summer

farmers   nervous   corner   north   normal

(*b*) A large initial hook, written on the inside of curves, forms the double consonants *fl, vl,* etc.

fly   flat   flowers   evil   civil   arrival

approval   beautiful   delightful   final

finally   original   originally   privilege

personal   personally   travel

SHORT FORMS

nor, or *in our*   near   own   owner   more

remark, or remarked   remarkable   *Mr. or mere*   sure

pleasure   larger   largely   everything   over

however   respectfully

EXERCISE 77

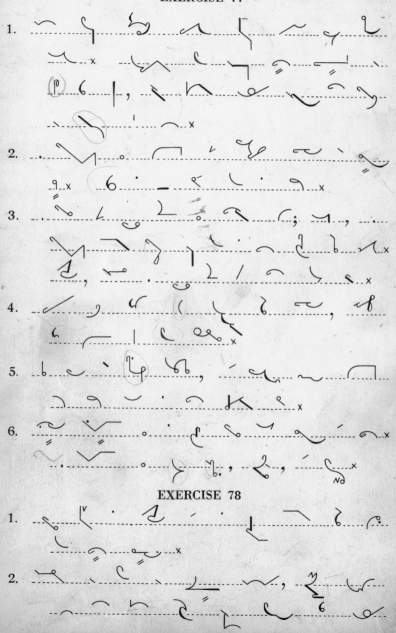

EXERCISE 78

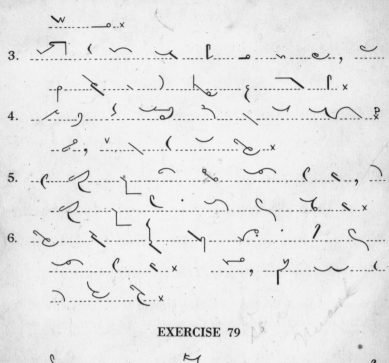

EXERCISE 79

(157)

43. Additional Forms

(*a*) The double consonants *fr, vr, thr,* and *THr,* are represented

by ⌐⌐ *fr* ⌐⌐ *vr* ⌐⌐ *thr* ⌐⌐ *THr* (reverse forms), as well as by

⌐⌐ *fr* ⌐⌐ *vr* ⌐⌐ *thr* ⌐⌐ *THr* (original forms).

When one of these double consonant strokes is the only stroke in the word, the reverse form is used *if the word does not begin with a vowel:*

⌐⌐ *free* ⌐⌐ *freight* ⌐⌐ *fruit* ⌐⌐ *three* ⌐⌐ *through*

but ⌐⌐ *either* ⌐⌐ *ever* ⌐⌐ *offer* ⌐⌐ *offered* ⌐⌐ *other*

(*b*) When joined to another stroke, the forms are used which join most conveniently. Usually, the reverse forms are joined to strokes written towards the right:

⌐⌐ *before* ⌐⌐ *bother* ⌐⌐ *leather* ⌐⌐ *brother* ⌐⌐ *cover*

⌐⌐ *covered* ⌐⌐ *discover* ⌐⌐ *forgot* ⌐⌐ *gather* ⌐⌐ *lever*

⌐⌐ *Denver*

NOTE: ⌐⌐ *Thursday* ⌐⌐ *thirty* ⌐⌐ *fresh*

(*c*) After *k, g, n,* or a straight upstroke, *fl* and *vl* are reversed:

rifle reflect naval novel rival

44. The double consonant stroke *shl* is always written upward. The stroke *shr* is always written downward:

official shelf partial specialize specialty

essential artificial pressure Fisher

45. The heavy sign is used to represent *ng-kr* or *ng-gr:*

thinker banker conquer finger stronger

SHORT FORMS

from very they are their, there

EXERCISE 80

1.

2.

3.

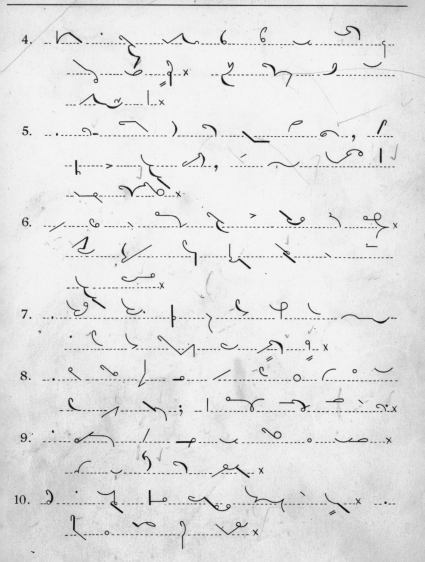

EXERCISE 81

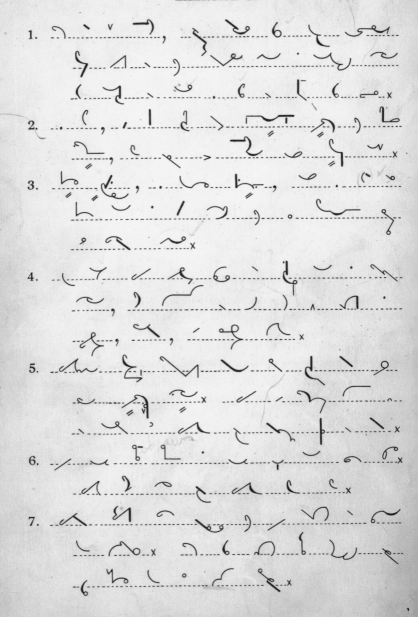

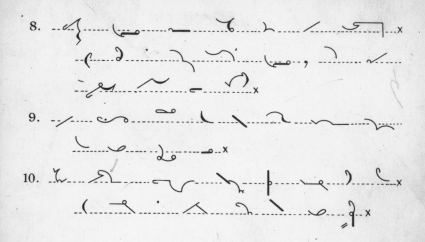

8. ...x

9. ...x

10. ...x

EXERCISE 82
(*Write in Shorthand*)

Frost Brothers, 120 Jefferson Avenue, Denver, Colorado.

Dear-Sirs: *We-are* afraid *that-it*-will-not-*be* possible *to*-recover-*the* total sum due *on-your* claim unless *you* adopt *different* measures. *We-have* used *special* efforts, *but* up *to-the* present *we-have* met *with* no success *in-our* endeavors *to-get-the* debtor *to* settle. *We-are*-unable-*to* collect *any* money, *nor can-we* extract *any* promise *from-him*.

We-think-you-will-be-obliged finally *to* pass-*the* claim *over to-your* attorneys. Please notify us if-*you wish-us to* proceed *with-the* case *and* take *this* step *for-you*. *Very*-truly-*yours*, (100)

CHAPTER XII

46. N Hook

(a) A small final hook, written on the inside of curves, adds *n*:

fine   phone   often   even   seven   than

then   zone   shown   machine   man   men

mean   remain   salesman   mine   nine   none

known   line   loan   iron   earn   women

(b) The *n* hook is written on the non-circle side of all straight strokes:

pen   pain   open   plan   brown   ten

ton   retain   gotten   forgotten   fifteen

bulletin   done   pardon   drawn   kitchen

join   June   imagine   clean   American

taken   gone   green   begin   rain   run

one   everyone   win   between   children

Final *r,* when hooked, is usually written upward:

turn   return   learn   western   corn   pattern

SHORT FORMS

been   general, or generally   within   southern

northern   opinion

Phrases: had been   have been   more than   better

than   larger than   smaller than   our own   their own

EXERCISE 83

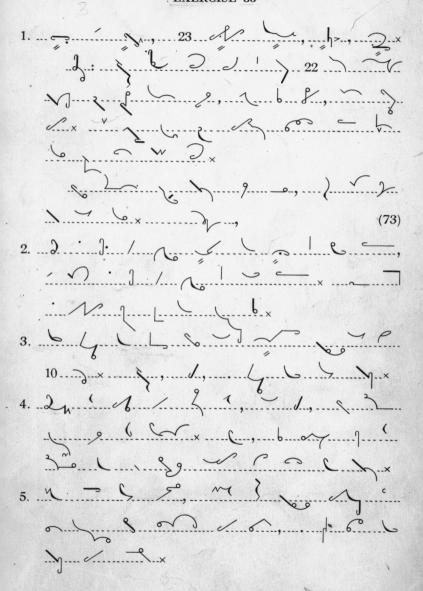

1.

23

22

(73)

2.

3.

10

4.

5.

EXERCISE 84

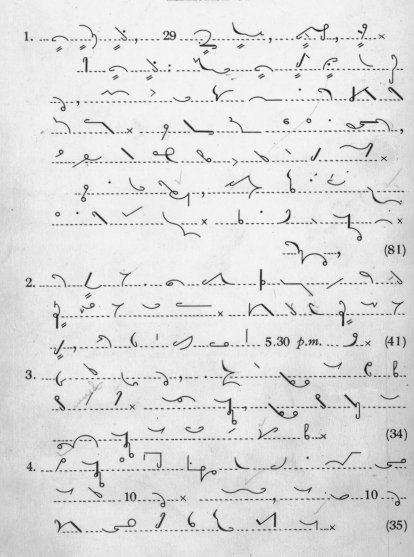

1. ... 29 ... (81)

2. ... 5.30 *p.m.* ... (41)

3. ... (34)

4. ... 10 ... 10 ... (35)

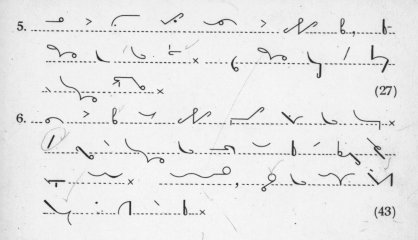

5. ... (27)

6. ... (43)

47. *F* or *V* Hook

A small final hook, written on the circle side of all straight strokes, adds *f* or *v*:

brief ... proof, or prove ... approve ... above ... active

relative ... attractive ... drive ... achieve ... gave

rough ... serve ... deserve ... preserve ... reserve

wife ... half

There is no *f* or *v* hook to curves.

SHORT FORMS

represent, or represented ... representative ... behalf

advantage ... Phrases: ... out of ... number of

instead of ... which have ... who have

EXERCISE 85

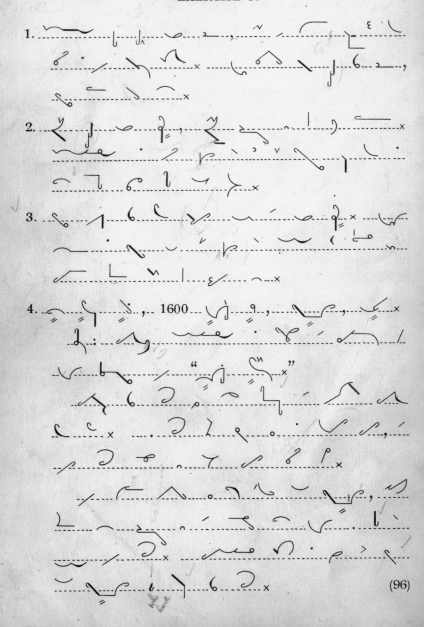

1.

2.

3.

4. 1600

EXERCISE 86

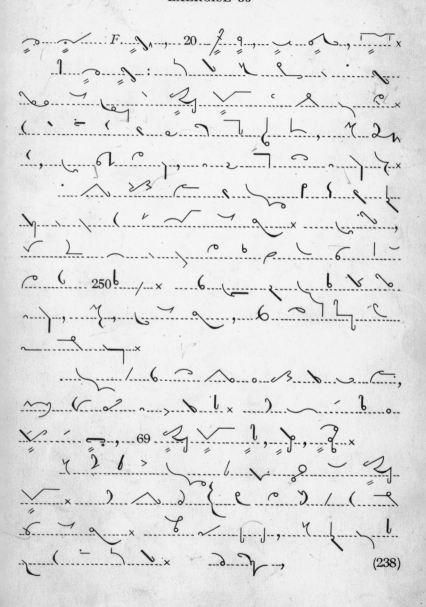

(238)

48. A finally hooked stroke is halved to indicate a following *t* or *d*:

(*a*)   find   found   event   meant, or mend   demand

mind   amount   moment   statement   payment

movement   settlement   shipment   friend   front

department   land   around

(*b*)   opened   band   print   plant, or planned

spent, or spend   point   pound   bound   attend

extent, or extend   instant   assistant   stand

president   kind   count   account   discount

second   grand   inclined   went   want

turned   current   round   returned

(*c*)   approved   gift   served   draft   achieved

deserved   reserved   observed

SHORT FORMS

gentleman   gentlemen   cannot   told   tried

trade   toward   third

Phrases: had not, or do not   did not

If it is necessary to indicate in your shorthand notes that a longhand abbreviation is to be used, write a fully vocalized outline for the abbreviation:

hadn't   don't   didn't   doesn't   haven't

won't   isn't   couldn't   can't

NOTE: can not (separate words)

EXERCISE 87

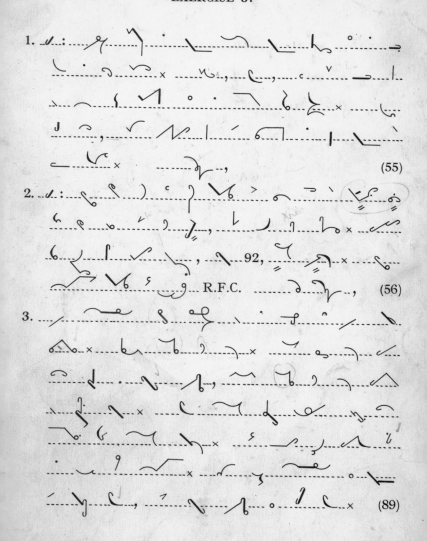

1. ... (55)

2. ... 92, ... R.F.C. ... (56)

3. ... (89)

EXERCISE 88

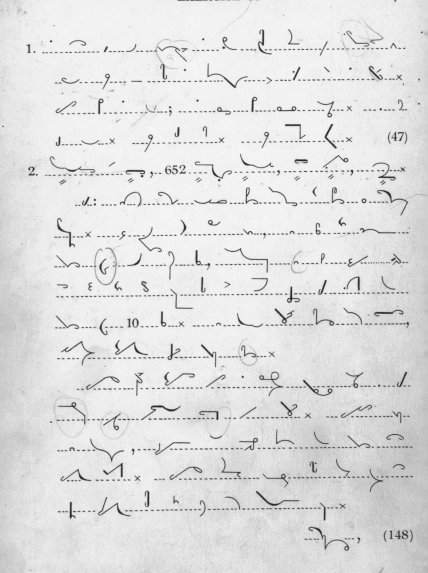

EXERCISE 89
(*Write in Shorthand*)

Bayne Brothers, 26 Lexington Avenue, Boston, Massachusetts.

Gentlemen: Please *be* kind-enough *to* supply-*the* items *on-the* attached list *as-soon-as*-possible. At-*the* present moment *there-is an* active demand *for-them, and-we*-hope *that-we-can* count *on having them within* three days. *In-the* event *that-you-cannot* supply *them within that*-time, please-*inform*-us by return mail.

Please-note-*that-the* exact items specified *are to-be* supplied. If-*you-are* out-*of* stock *of any of-the* items, *do*-not supply *different* articles. *Anything that-is*-not exactly *as* specified must *be* returned.

We-enclose *our* check for $65 *which-is to-be* applied *toward our* account. *Yours*-truly, (112)

49. The final hooks are used in the middle of a word when they join easily to the following strokes:

(*a*) ⟋ *evening* ⟋ *finance* ⟋ *arrange* ⟋ *arrangement*

⟍ *opening* ⟍ *planning* ⟍ *training* ⟍ *attended*

⟍ *splendid* ⟍ *extended* ⟍ *merchandise* ⟍ *hundred*

⟍ *beginning*

(*b*) ⟍ *perfect* ⟍ *profit* ⟍ *provide* ⟍ *provided* ⟍ *private*

⟍ *advance* ⟍ *definite* ⟍ *definitely* ⟍ *telephone* ⟍ *refer*

⟍ *prefer*

(*c*) ⟍ *pointing* ⟍ *standing* ⟍ *spending* ⟍ *finding*

⟍ *printing* ⟍ *amounting* ⟍ *mountain* ⟍ *extending*

⟍ *apparently* ⟍ *memorandum* ⟍ *correspondence*

⟍ *country* ⟍ *kindly* ⟍ *kindness*

but note: ⌒˙ *wanted* ⌒⸜ *printed* ⌒ᵥ *meantime* ⌒˙ *seconded*

⌒˙ *accounted*

EXERCISE 90

1. ⟍: .... (52)

2. ⟍: .... (68)

EXERCISE 91

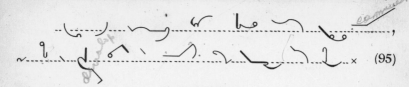

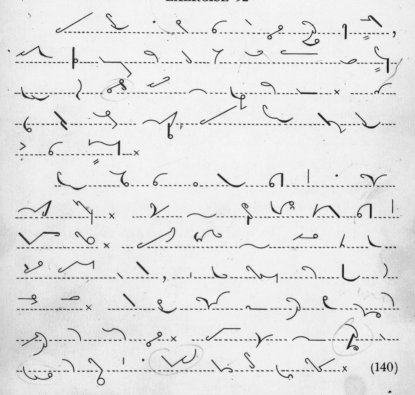

EXERCISE 92

(95)

(140)

50. Final *s* circle is written inside the *f* or *v* hook:

proofs, or *proves*   *relatives*   *drafts*   *achieves*

deserves   *reserves*   *wives*   *gifts*

representatives   *advantages*

51. A final circle, or a final loop, written on the same side of a straight stroke as the *n* hook, includes the *n:*

chance   chances   expense   expenses   distance

dance   dances   danced   plans   instance

instances   turns   returns   once   accounts

against   bonds   wants   attends   pounds

stands   students   depends   reference   references

52. The small circle is written inside the *n* hook attached to curves, and adds the final sound *z* only:

means   remains   loans   funds   friends

earns   women's   events   demands

53. After a curved stroke the light sound *-nce* is represented by stroke *n* and the final *s* circle:

offence   announce   allowance   romance

offences   fenced   announced   announces

announcing   allow   allowances

54. When a vowel follows *f, v,* or *n,* at the end of a word, it is necessary to write the stroke in order to place the vowel sign:

coffee   cough   funny   fun   county   count

penny   pen   review   rough

SHORT FORMS

difficult   difficulty   balance   balanced

responsible   great   guard   gold

Phrase: at once

EXERCISE 93

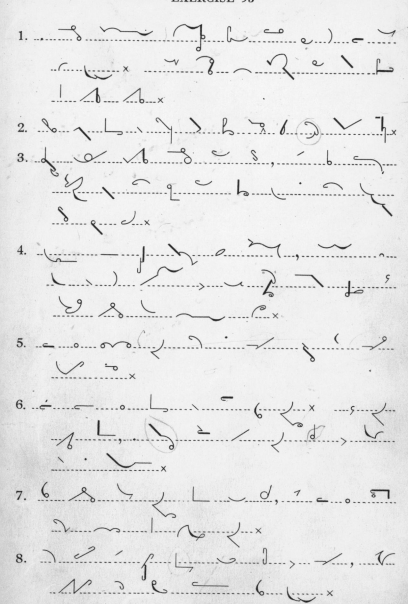

EXERCISE 94

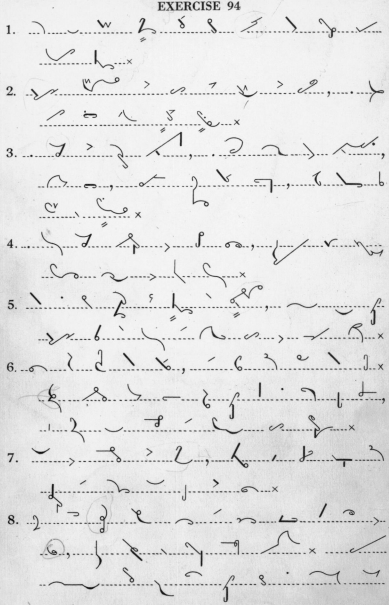

EXERCISE 95

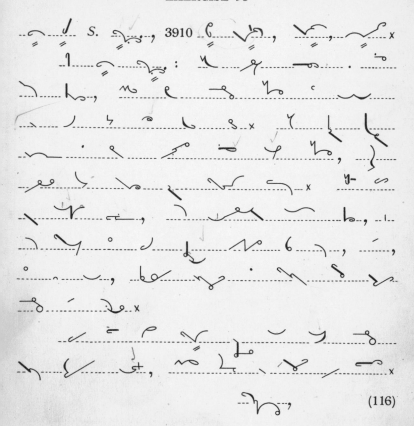

(116)

EXERCISE 96

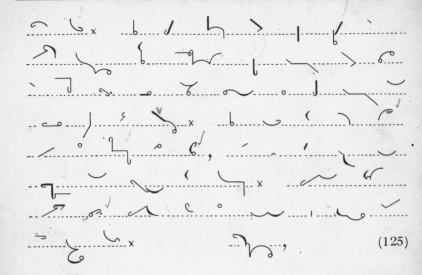

(125)

EXERCISE 97
(*Write in Shorthand*)

1. *This* firm furnished excellent references, so *we-think-we should* extend-*the* time *for*-payment *of-the balance* due *on-their*-account.

2. *The young*-man stands *a very*-good chance *of* obtaining-*the* post *of* assistant manager *of-the* bond department *owing to-the* splendid training he-*has* received.

3. Please provide us *with a* memorandum *of all* merchandise *which-is subject to a special* allowance.

4. *The* rough draft serves *to* show *how-the* use *of-the* telephone *has-been* extended *during-the* last seven *years*.

5. *Several of-the* students *have-been* taken out-*of-the* second grade, *and-we* plan *to*-make other arrangements *for-those-who* remain.

6. *Your* statement *is* returned *because-the* amount *of-the* discount *which-you have* deducted *is*-not correct.

EXERCISE 98

(*Write in Shorthand*)

Messrs. Evans *and* Groves, 46 West *Third* Street, Houston, Texas.

Gentlemen: We would-be ungrateful indeed if-*we*-did-not accept *your* kind hint. *As a* direct result *we-have* planned *a* series *of* trips *for our representatives which-will* bring *them into* closer touch *with our* customers *all-over-the* United-States. *Our* men leave New-York at-once *with* samples *of-our* advance lines. They-will explain *to-you-the* reasons *for-the* apparent slackness *we-have* shown *during-the* past season. *It-has-been* one *of-much* stress *for*-us, *and-we-are*-inclined-*to-think you*-will make-*the* proper allowances *when-you* learn-*the* reason.

You-will-*be*-glad *to* know *that-the* new lines *to-be* shown *to-you have-been* favorably received *in-the northern* states. They-*are of* splendid value, *and are* sold at-prices *that give*-us *a very*-low margin *of*-profit. *Yours very*-truly, (144)

CHAPTER XIII

55. -*Shun* Hook

A large final hook adds the final syllable -*shun*. This large hook is written on the inside of curves:

fashion *motion* *nation* *relation* *attention*

examination *session* *division* *explanation*

extension *profession* *supervision* *mention*

admission *expansion* *intention*

The *s* circle is added as shown: *fashions* *nations* *relations*

When a good joining is obtained, the large hook is used when the -*shun* syllable occurs in the middle of a word:

national *professional* *intentional*

EXERCISE 99

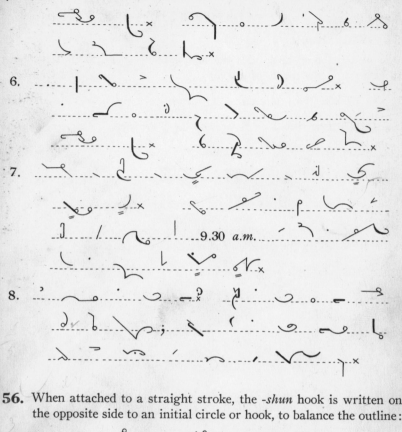

56. When attached to a straight stroke, the *-shun* hook is written on the opposite side to an initial circle or hook, to balance the outline:

section   station   exception   expression

transaction   reception   anticipation   discussion

recollection   registration   exceptionally

After _____ and _____ the *-shun* hook is written away from the curve, to balance the outline:

fiction   vacation   vocation   location   selection

vocational   affectionate

EXERCISE 100

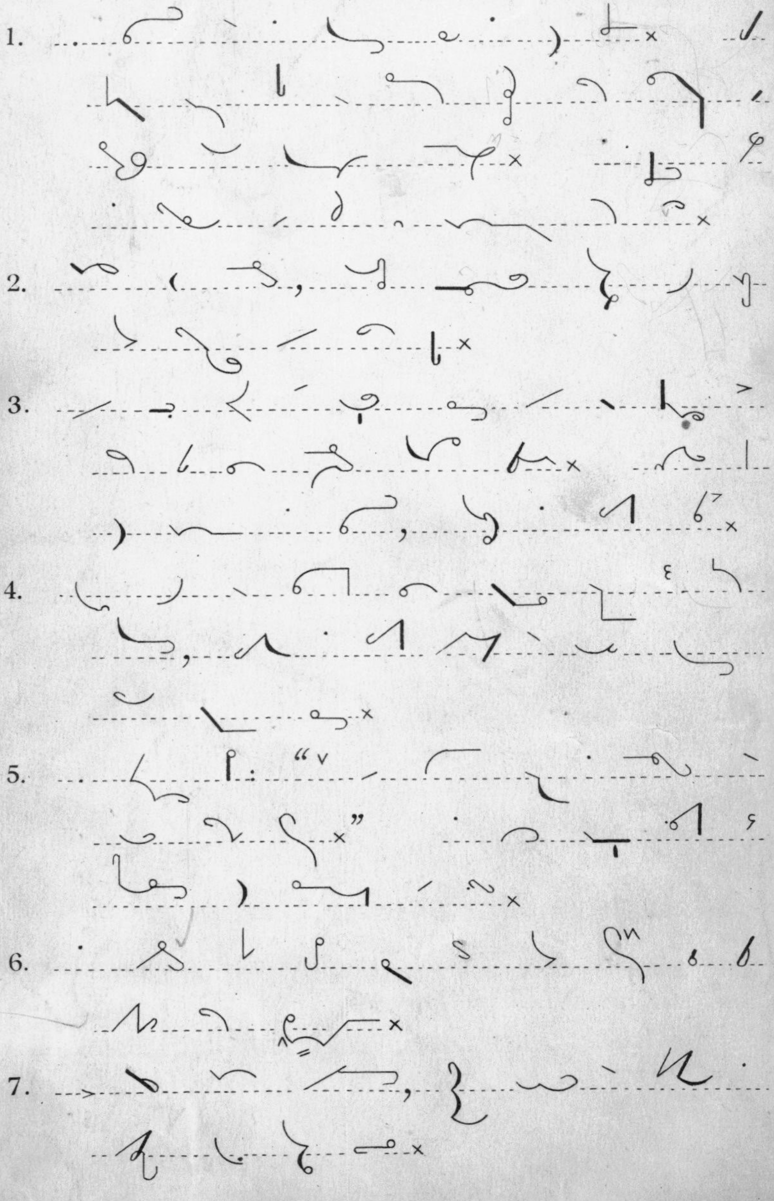

1. [shorthand outlines]

2. [shorthand outlines]

3. [shorthand outlines]

4. [shorthand outlines]

5. [shorthand outlines]

6. [shorthand outlines]

7. [shorthand outlines]

8.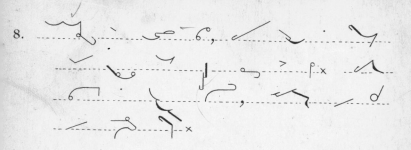

57. The -*shun* hook is written on the right side of simple *t, d,* or *j*:

notation   _invitation_   _expectation_   _imitation_

presentation   _reputation_   _petition_   _addition_

edition   _additional_   _magician_

When added to other simple straight strokes, -*shun* is written on the side opposite to the last vowel:

action   _caution_   _portion_   _operation_   _occasion_

education   _application_   _distribution_   _election_

direction   _attraction_   _deduction_   _obligation_

reduction   _occupation_   _educational_   _occasional_

occasionally

EXERCISE 101

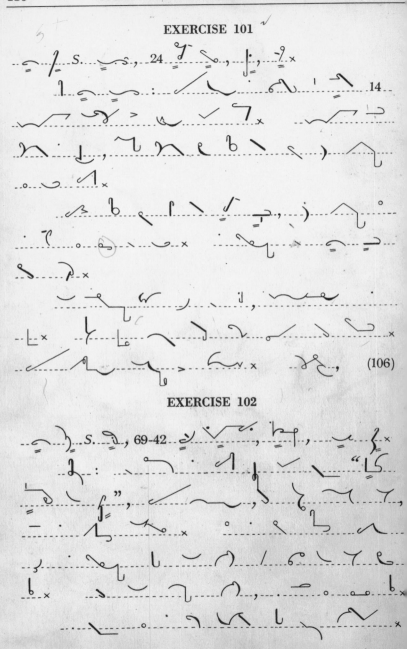

(106)

EXERCISE 102

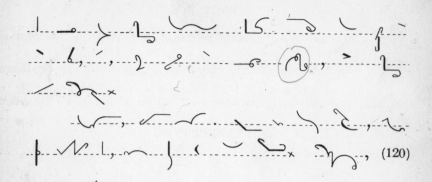

(120)

58. *S-Shun*

When *-shun* follows the *s* circle or the *ns* circle, it is represented by a small curl (a continuation of the circle). A third-place vowel between the *s* and *-shun* is placed outside the curl. Any other vowel is not indicated.

decision   *position*   *opposition*   *disposition*

proposition   *possession*   *taxation*   *physician*

musician   *succession*   *sensation*   *transition*

A final *s* circle is placed inside the curl:

possessions   *decisions*   *physicians*   *transitions*

59.
In words ending in *-uation* or *-uition,* the stroke *sh* and *n* hook are generally used:

situation   *tuition*

A stroke hooked for *-shun* is halved to indicate a final *t* or *d:*

motioned   *cautioned*   *fashioned*

SHORT FORMS

～ *information* ＼ *public, publish,* or *published* ＼ *publication*

＞ *object,* or *objected* ＞ *objection* ～ *organize,* or *organized*

～ *organization* ～ *satisfaction* ～ *investigation* ℰ *yesterday*

EXERCISE 103

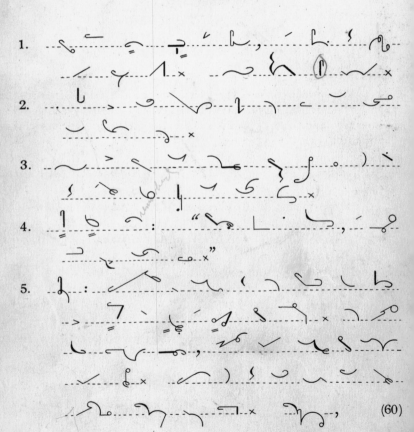

(60)

EXERCISE 104

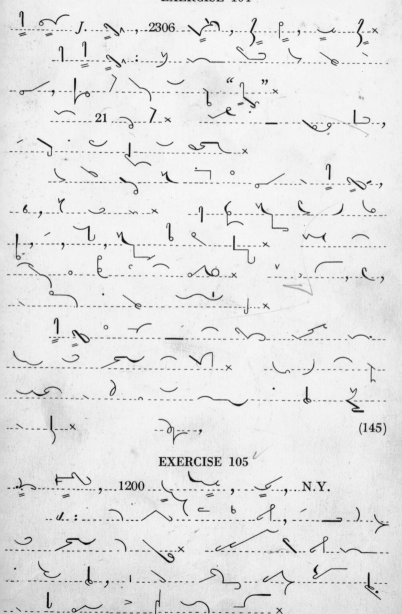

(145)

EXERCISE 105

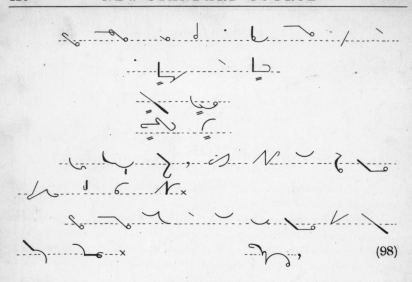

(98)

EXERCISE 106

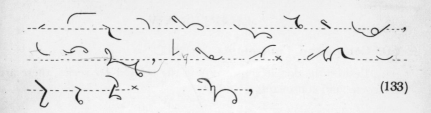

(133)

EXERCISE 107
(Write in Shorthand)

Muir *and* Richman, 6 College Street, New Haven, Connecticut.
Attention *of* Mr. Frank Smith.

Gentlemen: We-think-we-are in *a* position *to* assist *you to-tell in what* direction *your* promotion work may best *be* extended. *As you-are-*no-doubt aware, *our organization has-given* many *years of* attention *to-*problems *of* distribution *of-*every *description, and-the information in-our-*possession *is* nation wide *and* reliable.

*We-believe-that-you would-*find *a* discussion *of-the* problem *with our* Mr. Jones *of-*value *to-you.* He-will-*be-*glad *to-*receive *an* invitation *from-you to-call. Very-*truly-*yours,* (89)

EXERCISE 108
(Write in Shorthand)

Mr. James Merrigan, 42 St. Marks Place, Brooklyn, *New York.*

*Dear-*Sir: *With-the* small amount *of information in-our-*possession, *we-are-*unable-*to give-you* a definite decision *on-your* application *for* a loan. *You-*make no mention *at-all of any* provision *for* expansion at-*your* present location, *nor do-you tell-*us if-*you have any* intention *of-*taking *over-the* operation *of more* machines.

However, we-believe-that-the proposition *is* certainly worth discussion, *but, of-*course, action must wait *till-you* furnish us *with* additional *information* about *your* plans.

*We-*suggest *that-you call* at-*our* office sometime *during-the-next* few days, *to-*permit us *to-go over* every angle *of-the* situation *with-you. Yours-*truly, (114)

CHAPTER XIV

60. Compound Consonants

Besides the double consonants in the *pel* and *per* series, there are six compound consonants:

Letter	Sign	Name	As in
KW		kwa	quick request
GW		gwa	guava linguist
MP, MB		emp } emb }	camp embody
LR		ler	filler scholar
RR		rer	poorer sharer
WH		hwa	where whip

1. quickly   quit   quote   quoted   quoting quarter   quantity   acquaintance   acquainted equipment   banquet   inquiry   request requested   require   requirements   square exquisite   adequate   Maguire   linguist

2. camp   campaign   stamp   dump   lump sympathy   embody   impose   imposes imposition

3. ⟍ roller ⟍ counsellor ⟍ ruler ⟍ scholars

4. ⟍ bearer ⟍ fairer ⟍ admirer ⟍ poorer ⟍ sharer

⟍ wearer

5. ⟍ where ⟍ white ⟍ somewhere ⟍ anywhere

⟍ nowhere ⟍ everywhere ⟍ elsewhere

When *m* is immediately followed by *pr, br, pl,* or *bl,* the double consonant strokes ⟍ ⟍ ⟍ ⟍ are used:

⟍ impress ⟍ embrace ⟍ imply ⟍ emblem

Ler is used only where the downward *l* would be used; *rer* is used only where the downward *r* would be used.

SHORT FORMS

⟍ whether ⟍ important, or importance ⟍ improve, improved,

or *improvement* ⟍ impossible ⟍ accord, according, or according to

⟍ cared ⟍ particular ⟍ opportunity

EXERCISE 109

1.

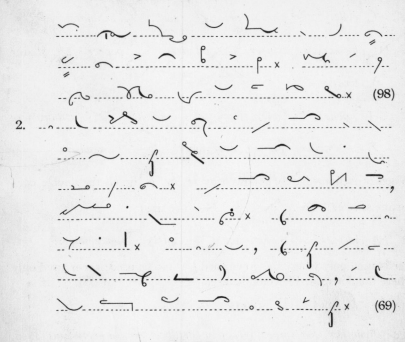

(98)

2.

(69)

EXERCISE 110

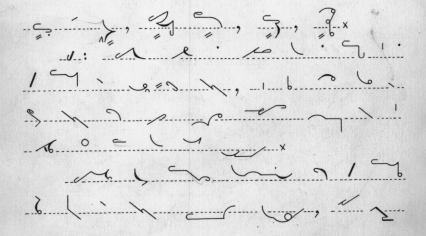

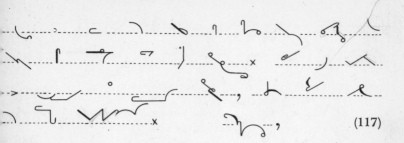

(117)

EXERCISE 111

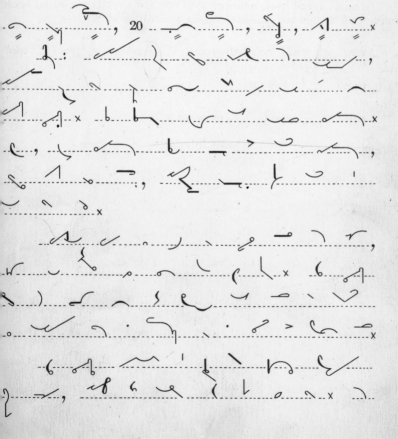

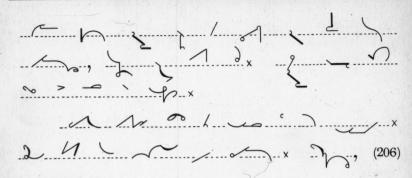

(206)

61. *Wl* and *Whl*

A small initial hook prefixes *w* to upward *l*. A large initial hook prefixes *wh* to upward *l*. These hooks are read first:

..⌒.. well ..⌒.. will ⌒.. willing ⌒.. unwilling ⌒.. wild ⌒.. wall

..⌒.. wealth ..⌒.. Walton

⌒.. while ..⌒.. wheel ..⌒.. meanwhile

EXERCISE 112

1.

(40)

2.

(50)

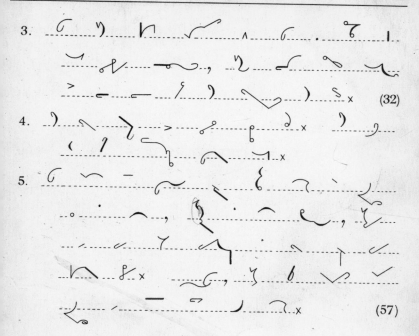

3.

4.

5.

(32)

(57)

62. Tick and Dot *H*

Generally the upward form of *h* is used when this stroke is joined to other consonants. When *h* is the only consonant, or when it is followed by *k* or *g*, the downward form is used:

he   *hug*   *hog*   *hook*   *Hague*

(*a*) The upward form is used for half-length *h* standing alone:

hate   *hot*   *hat*   *heat*   *height*

(*b*) A small tick, written as shown, represents *h* before *m, l,* and downward *r:*

home   *whom*   *Hamilton*   *hall*   *health*   *hello*

help   *hold*   *holiday*   *hair*   *hear, or here*

her   *herself*   *horse*   *hurt*   *harm*

(c) Where it would be awkward to write the stroke *h* in the middle of a word, *h* is represented by a light dot placed alongside the vowel sound, as shown:

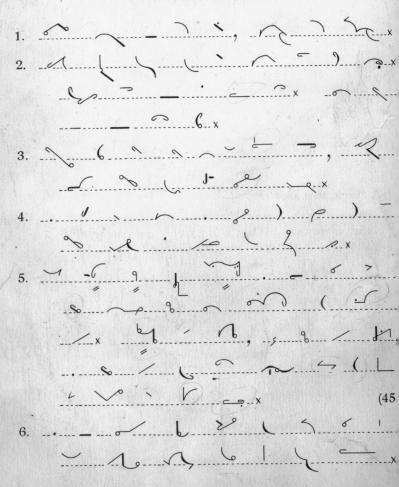

perhaps   *neighborhood*   *likelihood*   *househo*

Manhattan

EXERCISE 113

1.

2.

3.

4.

5.

(45

6.

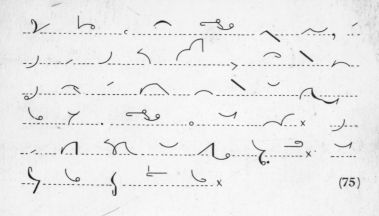

(75)

3. Contractions

Where a consonant is only lightly sounded in certain cases it is omitted:

postpone *postage* *postal* *post office* *mostly*

honestly *substitute* *institute* *institution*

adjustment *mistake* *mistaken* *investigate*

anxious *anxiously* *distinct* *distinction*

prompt *stamped*

EXERCISE 114

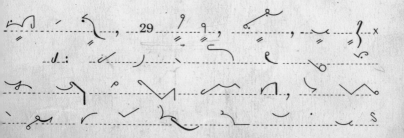

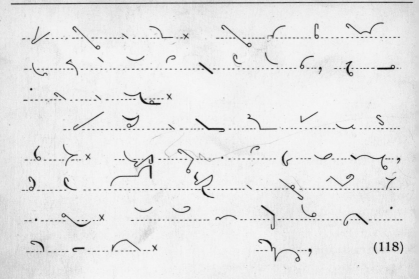

(118)

EXERCISE 115

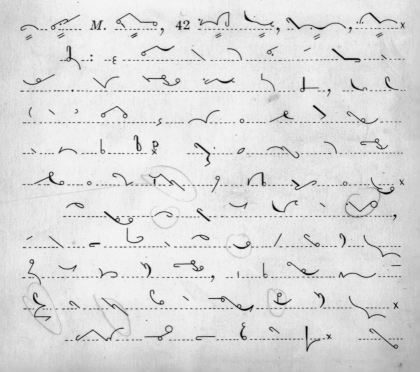

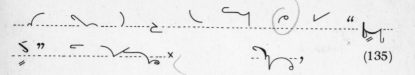

(135)

EXERCISE 116
(*Write in Shorthand*)

1. Henry R. Waters &-Sons, 642 Harrison Avenue, Cleveland, Ohio.

Gentlemen: We-are anxious *to*-receive-*the* package *of* pens *which ac-cording-to your* invoice *of November* 14 *was sent* by-mail five days ago. *We*-presume *that-the* package *was sent* by registered mail.

In-answer *to-our* inquiry, *the* post-office here says *that-the* package *has*-not-yet-*been* received. *Do-you think that-there-has-been a* mistake *in* addressing-*the* package? *Yours very*-truly, (69)

2. Hamilton *&* Hickey, 20 Grand Street, Rochester, New-York.

Gentlemen: We-are-sorry *to*-learn *that-the* package *we-sent to-you* by registered mail *on* November 14 *has*-not-*been* received. Promptly upon receipt *of-your* note *we-sent a* duplicate package.

It-is-possible, *of*-course, *that-the* package *was* incorrectly addressed, *but-we-do-not-think that-there-is any* likelihood *that-this-is-the* case. *We-are* asking-*the* postal authorities *to* institute *a* search *for-the* lost package, *and*-no-doubt they-will-*be*-able-*to* find *it*.

Meanwhile, if-*the* original package *is delivered to-you,* will-*you*-kindly return *it to*-us. *The* cost *of* postage will-*be-sent to-you,* or *you-can* make *an* adjustment *in-your*-account *when-you* mail *your* check. *Very*-truly-*yours*, (126)

CHAPTER XV

64. Halving

There are a few additional applications of the halving princi

(a) The strokes *m* and *n* are halved and thickened to indicate a 1 lowing *d*:

⌒ made   ⌒ mad   ⌒ madam   ⌒ moderate   mod

⌒ middle   seemed   named   ashamed   assur

end   send   signed   sound   intend   thous

designed   telephoned   indicate   undoubt

need

(b) Downward *l* and downward *r* are halved and thickened to indi a following *d*:

billed   mailed   child   field   old   w

filed   detailed   yield   failed   inste

board   appeared   afford   desired   acqu

card   insured   assured   heard   ve

standard   ordinary

EXERCISE 117

1.

2.

3.

4.

5.

6.

(95)

65. Final *lt* is expressed by ‿⌒ , and final *rt* is generally expresse

by ‿⌒ :

⟋⌒ *belt* ⟍⌒ *felt* ‿⟍ *built* ⌣ *fault* ⟍⌢ *bolts* ⌐ *star*

⟍⌒ *support* ‿⌣ *smart* ⟍ *sort* ‿⌿ *skirt* ‿⟍ *part* ⟍⌣ *por*

⟍⌣ *sport* ⟋⟍⌣ *report* ‿⟍⌣ *export* ‿⌒⌣ *import*

66. When a vowel comes between *l-d* or *r-d*, the full strokes must t

written:

‿⌒╱ *carried* ⌐╱ *delayed* ⌣╱ *followed* ‿⌒╱ *married* ⌣╱ *value*

⌣╱ *borrowed* ⟍╱ *worried*

67. As indicated in paragraph 35b, strokes of unequal length mu

not be joined if their length would not clearly show. To show the di

ference in length, disjoin half length *t* or *d* following stroke *t* or *d*:

⌐ *attitude* ⌐⌐ *credited* ╷ *treated* ‿⌐ *dictated*

╷ *straightened* ‿⌢╷ *illustrated* ⟍╷ *postdated*

Special use of disjoining: ‿⌒ *promptness* ‿⌐ *indebtedness* ‿⌐ *out*

SHORT FORMS

⌐ *short* ‿ *hand* ‿ *under* ⌐ *yard* ⌐ *word* ‿⌒ *immedia*

‿⌒ *school* ‿⌒ *schooled* ‿ *spirit* ‿⌒ *certificate* ⌐ *knowled*

‿⌒ *acknowledge*

The halving principle is used to form the phrases ‿⌐ *if it* ‿⌐ *if it*

‿⌐ *in which it is* ⌐ *I am not* ‿⌢ *you are not* ‿⌒ *you will*

‿⌣ *you were not* ‿⌣ *this would be*

EXERCISE 118

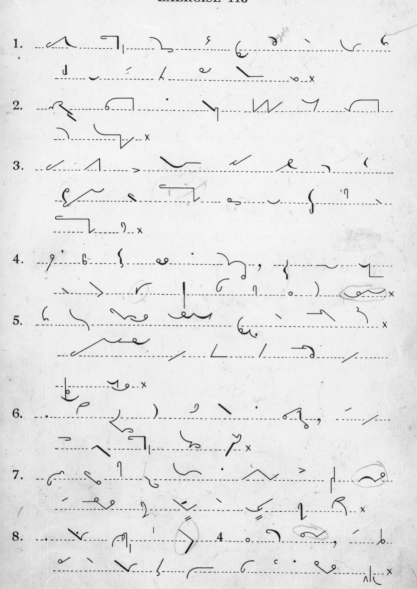

EXERCISE 119

1.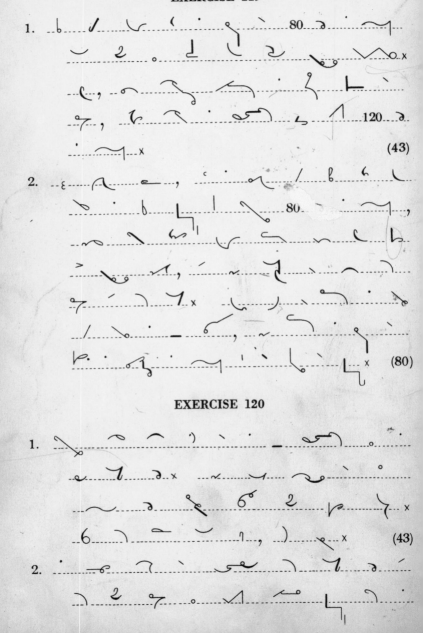

(43)

2.

(80)

EXERCISE 120

1.

(43)

2.

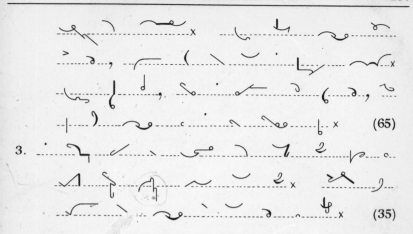

(65)

3.

(35)

EXERCISE 121

J. M. , 62 , , x

, (110)

EXERCISE 122

(Write in Shorthand)

Smart *and* Walsh, 62 *School* Street, Portland, Oregon.

Gentlemen: Please-*inform*-us *immediately when-we*-may *expect-the* lighting fixtures *we* ordered *from-you on* October 7, *for-the* apartmen house *we-are*-now *building. According-to* our *under*standing at *that* time, *you*-were *to-deliver them towards-the* end *of-the*-month, *but-yor have* failed *to do*-so.

It-is distinctly *under*stood, *of*-course, *that-the* delay *is*-not intentiona *on-your* part, *but-we-have* received no *word from-you.* Please-*do*-no hesitate *to inform*-us if-*you-are*-not able-*to*-make *immediate delivery We-think-you*-will-not mis*under*stand *our* attitude *when-we* say *tha* if-*you-cannot deliver-them immediately we-shall-have to*-get *them* else where. Work *is*-now *be*ing delayed, *and-we* simply *cannot* afford *to* wait. *Very*-truly-*yours,* (131)

68. Doubling Principle

Curved strokes are doubled in length to indicate a following syl lable *tr, dr,* or *THr:*

Stroke *l* standing alone, or with only a final *s* circle, is doubled to ad *tr* only:

EXERCISE 123

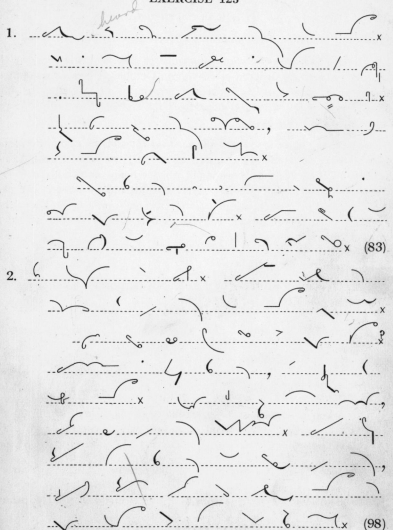

1.

(83)

2.

(98)

EXERCISE 124

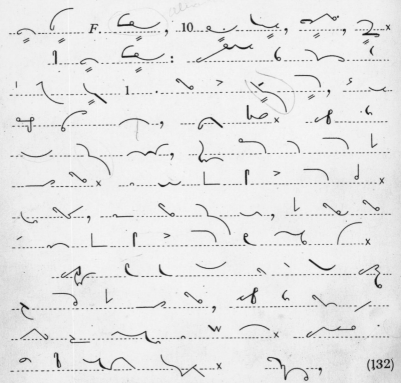

(132)

69. A straight stroke is doubled to indicate *tr, dr,* or *THr,* only

    (1) when it follows another stroke or circle *s,* or

    (2) when it has a finally joined diphthong or a final hook:

chapter   director   operator   educator

refrigerator   typewriter   scatter   powder

render   painter   tender   winter   wonder

renders   wonders, but   better   gather   weather

readers   platter   trader

70. In a few common words the syllable *-ture* is represented by the doubling principle:

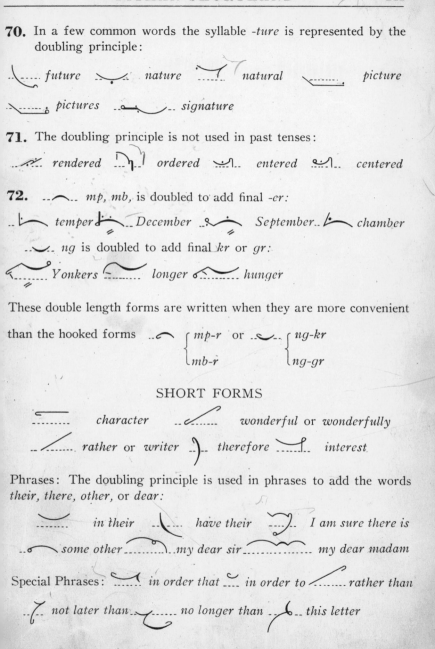

future   nature   natural   picture

pictures   signature

71. The doubling principle is not used in past tenses:

rendered   ordered   entered   centered

72. *mp, mb,* is doubled to add final *-er:*

temper   December   September   chamber

ng is doubled to add final *kr* or *gr:*

Yonkers   longer   hunger

These double length forms are written when they are more convenient

than the hooked forms   { *mp-r* or   { *ng-kr*
                             { *mb-r*   { *ng-gr*

SHORT FORMS

character   wonderful or wonderfully

rather or writer   therefore   interest

Phrases: The doubling principle is used in phrases to add the words *their, there, other,* or *dear:*

in their   have their   I am sure there is

some other   my dear sir   my dear madam

Special Phrases: in order that   in order to   rather than

not later than   no longer than   this letter

EXERCISE 125

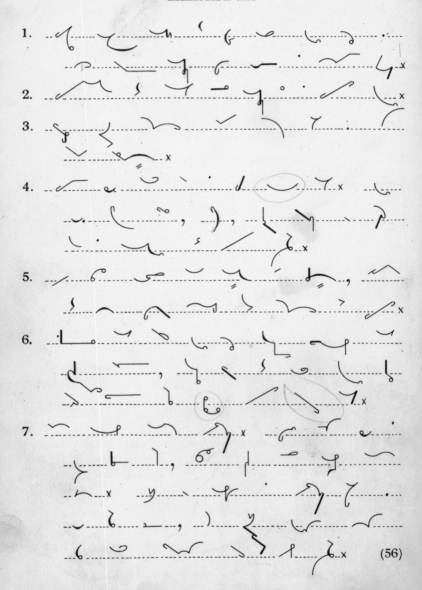

(56)

8.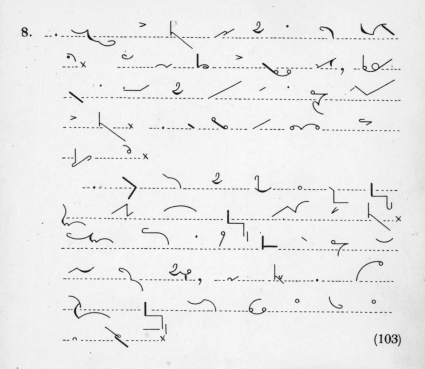

(103)

EXERCISE 126

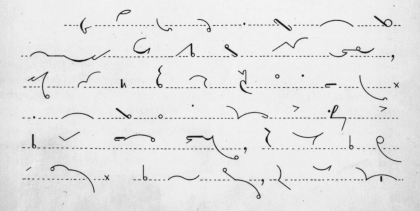

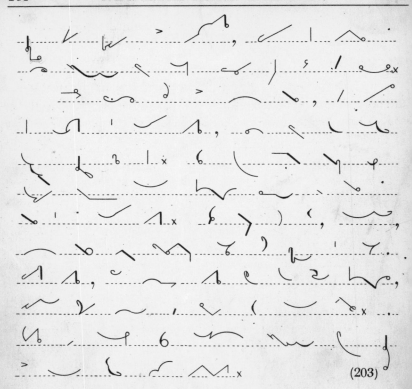

(203)

EXERCISE 127

(Write in Shorthand)

Mr. Alexander M. Porter, 129 *Third* Avenue, New-York, N. Y.

My-*dear*-Sir: *On behalf of-our*-clients, Messrs. Center *and* Walters, *who-have* requested us *to-represent their interests in-the*-matter *of-the* leasehold *on-the building* at 129 *Third* Avenue, *we-wish to inform-you that-we-have-their* permission *to* obtain *a* court order, *under-the* terms *of-which you*-will-not-*be*-able-*to* alter *the* front *of-the building.*

We-think-there-is no-doubt *that-the*-terms *of-the* lease *have-been* violated, *and in-our-opinion it*-will-*be to-your interest to* halt *any* further operations until *a* decision *has-been* rendered by-*the* court. *Very*-truly-*yours.* (108)

CHAPTER XVI

73. Prefixes

(a) The prefix *con-*, or *com-*, is expressed by a dot, written first at the beginning of an outline, as shown. In words beginning with the *con-* or *com-* dot, the first vowel after the prefix determines the position of the outline:

condition   conduct   confident   confidence

connect   connected   connection   consider

considerable   consideration   considered   considering

contained   consequently   comfortable   contents

continue   continued   convention   contract

concern   concerned   construction   conversation

contrary   company   committee   common

communication   community   comply   complete

completely   complaint

Special Forms: commerce   commission

(b) *Con-*, *com-*, *cum-*, or *cog-*, in the middle of a word or phrase is expressed by writing two strokes close to each other:

misconduct   disconnect   reconsider   discontinued

uncommon   discomfort   circumference   recognize

I am confident   you will be compelled

74. (*a*) *Accom-* or *accommo-* is expressed by........*k,* either joined or disjoined:

..........). *accomplish* ....). *accomplished* .... *accommodate* .... *accompany*

(*b*) *Intro-* is expressed by.........*ntr:*

.... *introduce* .... *introduced*

(*c*) *Magna-, magni-,* or *magne-,* is expressed by disjoined *m:*

.... *magnanimous* .... *magnificent* .... *magnitude* .... *magnetize*

EXERCISE 128

1.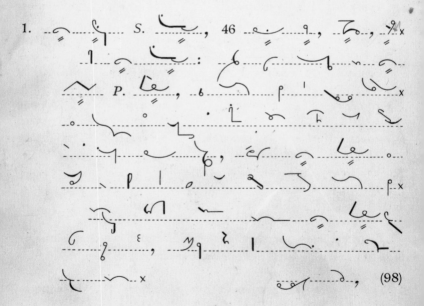

(98)

2. *(shorthand outlines)* , 14 *(shorthand outlines)* , *(shorthand outlines)* , D.C.

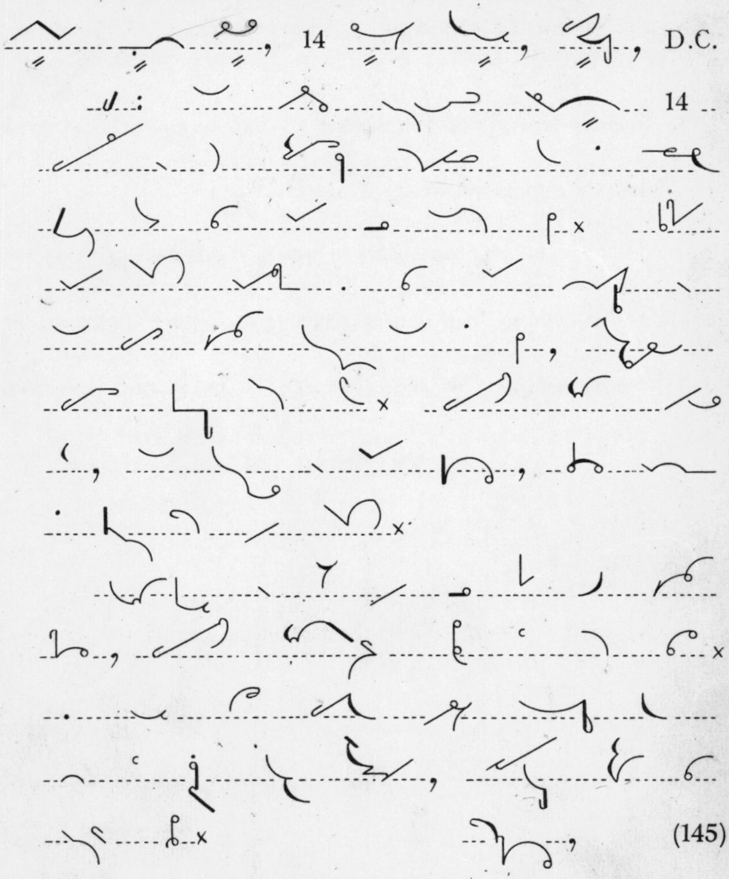

(shorthand outlines) 14

(shorthand outlines)

(shorthand outlines) x

(shorthand outlines)

(shorthand outlines) , *(shorthand outlines)*

(shorthand outlines) x *(shorthand outlines)*

(shorthand outlines) , *(shorthand outlines)* , *(shorthand outlines)*

(shorthand outlines) x

(shorthand outlines)

(shorthand outlines) , *(shorthand outlines)* x

(shorthand outlines)

(shorthand outlines) , *(shorthand outlines)* 6

(shorthand outlines) x (145)

75. (*a*) *Self-* is expressed by a disjoined *s* circle, and *self-con-* is represented by writing the *s* circle in the place of the *con-* dot:

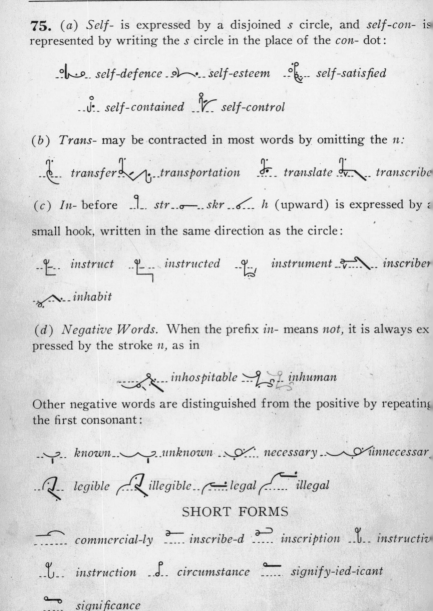

self-defence   self-esteem   self-satisfied

self-contained   self-control

(*b*) *Trans-* may be contracted in most words by omitting the *n*:

transfer   transportation   translate   transcribe

(*c*) *In-* before   *str*   *skr*   *h* (upward) is expressed by a small hook, written in the same direction as the circle:

instruct   instructed   instrument   inscribe

inhabit

(*d*) *Negative Words.* When the prefix *in-* means *not*, it is always expressed by the stroke *n*, as in

inhospitable   inhuman

Other negative words are distinguished from the positive by repeating the first consonant:

known   unknown   necessary   unnecessary

legible   illegible   legal   illegal

SHORT FORMS

commercial-ly   inscribe-d   inscription   instructive

instruction   circumstance   signify-ied-icant

significance

EXERCISE 129

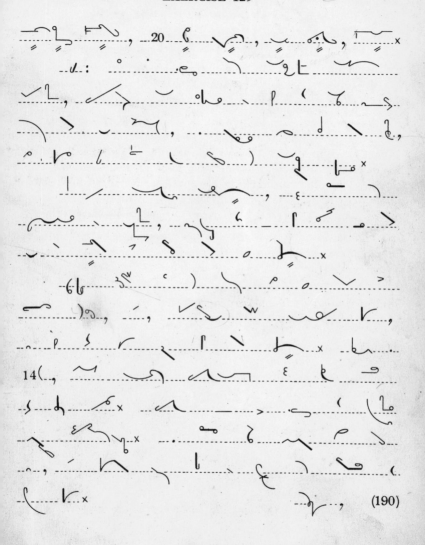

(190)

EXERCISE 130
(*Write in Shorthand*)

John S. Wilson & Company, *Northern* Avenue, Hartford, Connecticut. *Gentlemen: We*-received *your* communication *of-the* 14th, *in-which-you* complain *of-the* delay *in-the* completion *of-your* contract. *That-we-have* failed *to* accomplish *what we*-promised *we*-must admit, *and-we very*-much regret *our* failure.

We-are confident, *however, that-the* contract *could-have-been* completed *as* agreed upon *but for-the* recent trouble *with-the Commercial* Transport Committee, *which-was immediately responsible for-the* delay. *Their* decision interfered considerably *with our* business, *and-when-we* state *that* only thirty *of-our* transport men *have* continued at work, *we-think-you-will* recognize *how difficult it-has-been to* satisfy *our* customers.

It-is-unnecessary *for*-us *to*-add *that-we should* regret-*the* transfer *of-your* business, considering-*the* long connection between us, *and-the* cause *of-the* present interruption. *Very*-truly-*yours,* (139)

76. Suffixes and Word-endings

Where it would be awkward to write ⌣ *ng* at the end of a word, the suffix -*ing* is represented by a light dot:

requesting   *ordering*   *meeting*   *covering*   *serving*   *assisting*   *attempting*   *morning*   *wanting*   *running*

The dot -*ing* is used after downward *r* and a light straight downstroke:

securing   *assuring*   *hearing*   *bearing*   *getting*   *paying*   *teaching*   *eating*   *keeping*   *replying*   *shipping*   *sitting*   *stating*   *staying*   *trying*

Usually the dot *-ing* is used after a short form:

.... *coming* .... *giving* .... *thanking* .... *thinking*

.... *interesting*

Where *-ing* is represented by the dot, the plural *-ings* is represented by a light dash, as shown:

.... *meetings* .... *mornings* .... *hearings*

77. The suffix *-ment* is represented by .... *nt,* where the sign .... *mnt* cannot be easily joined:

.... *achievement* .... *consignment* .... *commencement*

.... *announcement*

(*a*) The suffix *-mental-ly-ity* is expressed by disjoined .... *mnt:*

.... *experimental* .... *departmental* .... *sentimental-ly-ity*

(*b*) The endings *-fulness* and *-lessness* are expressed by disjoined .... *fs,* and .... *ls* respectively:

.... *thoughtfulness* .... *thoughtlessness* .... *hopefulness*

.... *hopelessness*

(*c*) The suffix *-ship* is represented by a joined or disjoined .... *sh:*

.... *friendship* .... *citizenship* .... *hardship* .... *membership*

.... *ownership*

(*d*) -*Lity* or -*rity,* preceded by any vowel, is expressed by disjoining the preceding stroke:

   possi b ility   *ina b ility*   *desira b ility*   *lia b ility*

   for m ality   *regu l arity*   *simi l arity*   *ma j ority*

   mi n ority

(*e*) The endings -*logical-ly* are represented by disjoined *j:*

   biological-ly   *psychological-ly*   *physiological-ly*

(*f*) The word endings -*ward* and -*yard* are expressed by half length *w* and *y* respectively:

   forward   *forwarding*   *backward*   *backyard*

Note: *forwarded*

(*g*) -*ly* is represented by the stroke *l* (disjoined where necessary), and in some cases by the hooked form:

   fairly   *easily*   *friendly*   *instantly*   *particularly*

   differently   *cheaply*   *actively*   *deeply*

SHORT FORMS

   govern-ed   *government*   *advertise-d-ment*   *regular*

   probable-ly-ility   *individual-ly*   *prospect*   *whatever*

   whenever   *sufficient-ly-cy*

EXERCISE 131

1. [shorthand outlines] ×

2. [shorthand outlines]

[shorthand outlines] ×

[shorthand outlines] ×

3. [shorthand outlines]

[shorthand outlines]

[shorthand outlines] ×

[shorthand outlines] × (51)

4. [shorthand outlines]

[shorthand outlines], 36×

[shorthand outlines] ×

[shorthand outlines]

[shorthand outlines] ×

[shorthand outlines]

[shorthand outlines] × (69)

5. [shorthand outlines] ×

[shorthand outlines]

[shorthand outlines]

[shorthand outlines] ? × (34)

EXERCISE 132

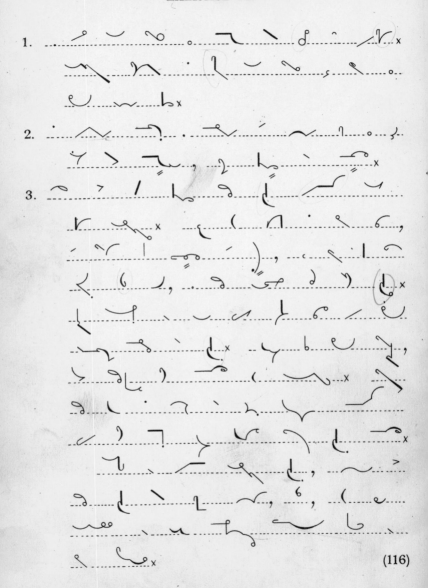

(116)

EXERCISE 133

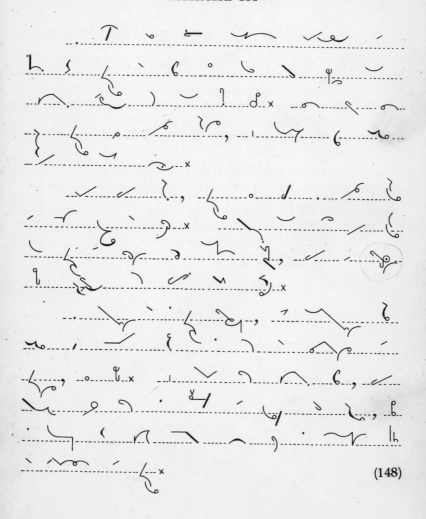

(148)

EXERCISE 134

(Write in Shorthand)

Mr. James T. Roberts, 29 Columbus Avenue, Yonkers, New-York.

Dear-Sir: *Your*-letter dated *the* 4th reached us *this* morning. *Your instructions have-been* noted, *but-we-are* afraid *that-it*-will-not-*be* possible *to*-make *all-the* alterations contained *in-your* memorandum *and-have-the* book ready by-*the* end *of-this* month. *However, we* fully recognize-*the* desirability *of-hav*ing-*the publication* completed at *an* early date, *and-we-are* requesting *our* printer *to* hasten-*the* setting *and* printing *as-much-as*-possible.·

The inscription will-be-placed after-*the* title page, *as you* desire. Proofs *of-the* last chapters will-*be* forwarded *to-you within a* few days.

Announcements will-*be published in next* Sunday's papers *to-the* effect *that a* new novel by *a* prominent *writer* will *short*ly appear. Please *tell*-us if-*you would rather have*-us use *your* name *in-the* announcement. *Very*-truly-*yours,* (142)

CHAPTER XVII

78. Diphones

Two consecutive vowels, pronounced in two separate syllables, are represented by the angular signs ⌐ ⌐ These signs are called *Diphones*.

The first ⌐ represents a dot vowel followed by any other vowel, and the second ⌐ represents a dash vowel followed by any other vowel. The signs are written in the place of the first vowel of the combination.

(1) _payable_ _saying_ _carrying_ _earlier_

earliest _idea_ _ideal_ _material_ _piano_

radio _previous_ _obvious_ _premium_

medium _really_ _real_ _realize_ _convenience_

convenient _experience_ _agreeable_ _glorious_

cordial _courteous_ _seeing_ _senior_ _serious_

studying _theater_ _various_

(2) _cooperate_ _cooperation_ _following_ _drawing_

growing _knowing_ _lower_ _lowest_ _poem_

showing _accruing_ _jewel_

79. The consecutive vowels in words like *question* are represented by the sign ⌐ :

question _union_ _suggestion_ _million_ _guardian_

80. Medial *W*

There is a small group of words in which *w* combined with a vowe
in the middle of a word is represented by a small semicircle. A left semi
circle represents *w* followed by a dot vowel, and a right semicircle
represents *w* followed by a dash vowel. The semicircles are written in
the place of the vowel with which the *w* is combined:

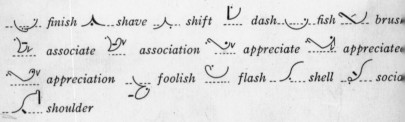

twelve   *twenty*   *frequently*   *herewith*

subsequent   *hardware*   *good will*

misquote   *guesswork*   *woodwork*

Special Forms: *quality*   *qualified*   *qualification*

somewhat

81. Upward *SH*

The stroke ⌐ *sh* is written upward in certain cases to obtain a
better outline:

finish   *shave*   *shift*   *dash*   *fish*   *brush*

associate   *association*   *appreciate*   *appreciated*

appreciation   *foolish*   *flash*   *shell*   *social*

shoulder

82. Stroke *R*

In order to keep the outline close to the line of writing, the upward
r is used where *r* follows two downstrokes, and, for the same reason,
downward *r* is used finally after two straight upstrokes:

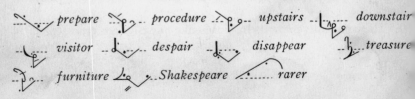

prepare   *procedure*   *upstairs*   *downstairs*

visitor   *despair*   *disappear*   *treasure*

furniture   *Shakespeare*   *rarer*

83. Stroke S

The stroke *s* is written (*a*) in words like 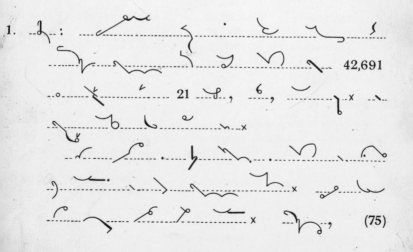 *science,* *scientific* *sighing* *Siam,* where a triphone immediately follows initial *s,* and (*b*) in words like *continuous* *fatuous* *strenuous* *pious,* where the final syllable *-ous* is immediately preceded by a diphthong.

SHORT FORMS

danger *financial-ly* *mortgage-d* *neglect-ed*

practice-d *university* *English* *exchange-d*

familiar-ity *telegram*

EXERCISE 135

1.

42,691

21

(75)

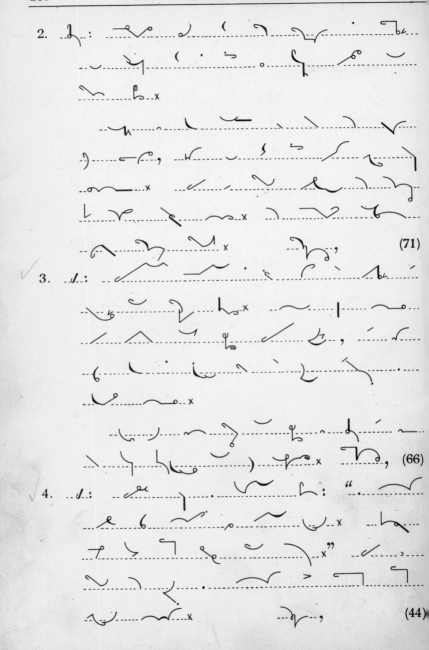

2.

(71)

3.

(66)

4.

(44)

5.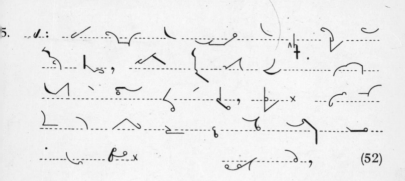

(52)

EXERCISE 136

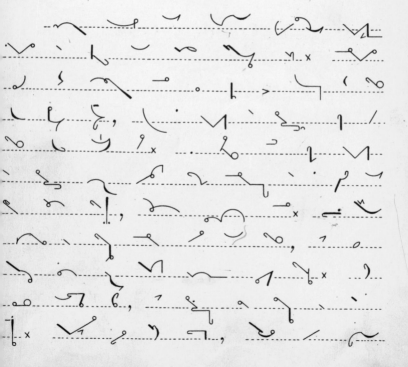

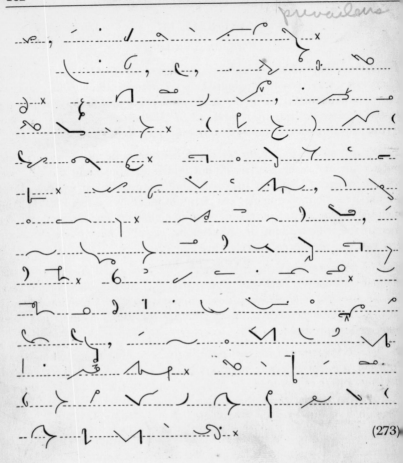

(273)

EXERCISE 137

(*Write in Shorthand*)

. William J. Anderson, *who-is* a professor *of English* at Columbia
University, has recently compiled *a* book *of* quotations *from* Shakespeare. *An* examination *of-the* book shows *that-we-do-*not-*have* to-go
o-*the* theater *to-*hear-*the language of* Shakespeare, *for-we* use *his*
erms *and-*phrases constantly *in-our* everyday speech. (53)

. *We-are* so *familiar with-the-*many conveniences *which* science *has*
ut within our reach *that-we-do-*not realize or appreciate *the* débt *we*
we to science. Constant use *and familiarity with-the* various time-
aving *and* labor-saving devices tend *to-*make-us *over*look *their* tre-
nendous value. *The* contributions *to-our* comfort *and* convenience by
nen *of* scientific training *are* continuous, *and-they-have* made-*the* mod-
rn world *a wonderful* place *to-*live *in.* (76)

. *The* treasurer prepares a statement *of-the financial* condition *of-the*
ompany annually. *This* statement *is usually* mailed *to-the* stockholders
n-*the* case *of a public* corporation. *A* comparison *with* previous annual
eports, or *balance* sheets, shows *whether-the year's trad*ing *has-been*
nore or less profitable. (48)

. *It-is-the practice of large insurance* firms *to* invest *the* bulk *of-their*
unds *in first mortgages on buildings,* homes, *and* farms. *It-is* considered
hat real estate *is* less liable *to* sudden changes *in* value, *and, therefore,*
here-is less *danger of-the* companies *hav*ing *to* suffer *any financial* loss
hrough a sudden drop *in-the* value *of-their* holdings. (62)

. *Dear-*Sir: Will-*you* please consider my application *for-the* position
f-treasurer *in-your organization. I-believe-that I-have-the* necessary
ualifications *and* experience, *and-I-*enclose a summary *of-them for-your*
nformation. If-*it-is* convenient, *I-shall* appreciate *an opportunity to*
iscuss my application *with-you, and any* questions *you-*may desire *to*
sk *can-be* answered fully *during-the* course *of-our* interview. *Yours-*
espectfully, (71)

CHAPTER XVIII

84. Figures

Figures *one* to *seven* and the figure *nine* are best represented by shorthand outlines. Other numbers, except round numbers, are represented by the ordinary Arabic numerals.

Round numbers are represented as follows:

for *hundred* or *hundredth;* ⟋ 700, ⟋ $200

⟍ or ⟍ for *thousand;* 5⟍ 5,000, 2⟍ $2,000, ⟍ 300,000

⟍ for *million;* ⟍ 4,000,000, ⟍ 200,000,000

⟍ for *billion;* 2⟍ *two billions*

85. Compound Words

Compounds of *here, there, where,* are written as follows:

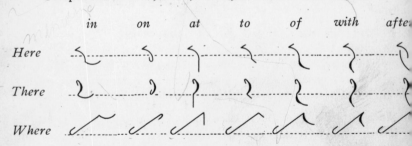

	in	*on*	*at*	*to*	*of*	*with*	*after*
Here							
There							
Where							

86. Intersections

The practice of intersecting one stroke through another is a very useful device for the representation of very commonly occurring phrases.

The device may be adapted to meet the special needs of the writer. Thus, for some shorthand writers the stroke *p* might usefully represent the word *party,* whereas in an insurance office the stroke *p* might better be used to represent *policy.*

Where intersection is not practicable, write one stroke close to another. The following list shows how the device may be used:

P	represents	*party*		Democratic Party
				Republican Party
B	"	*bank* or *bill*		bank rate
				city bank
				bill of lading
T	"	*attention*		early attention
				necessary attention
D	"	*department*		science department
				foreign department
CH	"	*charge*		this charge
				free of charge
J	"	*Journal*		Bankers' Journal
				Journal of Commerce
K	"	*company, cover,* or *captain*		this company
				under separate cover
				Captain Thompson
G	"	*government*		government official
				government office

F represents	*form*			necessary form
				as a matter of form
TH	"	*month*		in a month's time
				for a month
M	"	*manager, morning,* or *mark*		general manager
				Monday morning
				auditor's mark
N	"	*national*		national defence
				national affairs
RAY	"	*require-d-ment railway,* or *railroad*		you may require
				will be required
				your requirements
				Central Railroad
R	"	*arrange-d-ment*		please make arrangements
				we have arranged
Kr	"	*corporation,* or *colonel*		public corporation
				Colonel Alexander
Pr	"	*professor*		Professor Jackson

SHORT FORMS

inconvenience-t-ly   *distinguish-ed*   *income*   *become*

becoming   *welcome*   *nevertheless*

EXERCISE 138

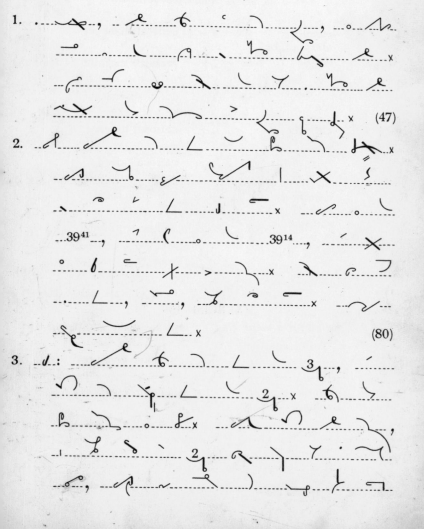

1.   (47)

2.   39⁴¹,   39¹⁴,   (80)

3.

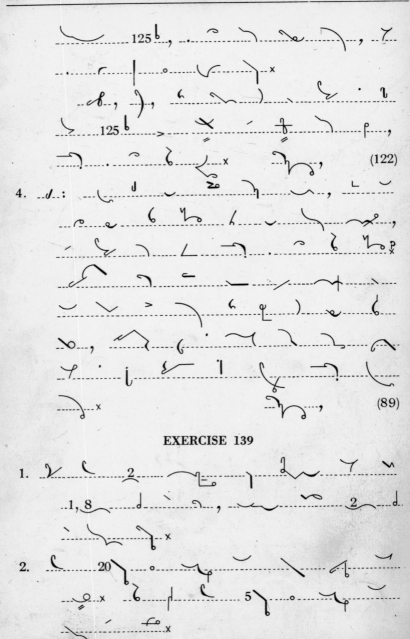

EXERCISE 139

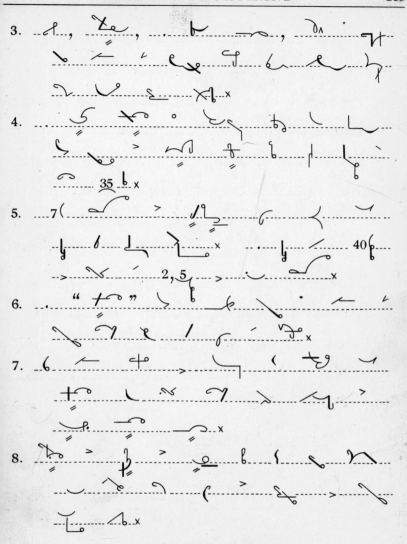

EXERCISE 140

[Shorthand outlines] 149(

[Shorthand outlines] 56, 5 ... x

[Shorthand outlines] 485

13 ... x   (74)

2. *[Shorthand outlines]*

[Shorthand outlines]

[Shorthand outlines]

[Shorthand outlines]

[Shorthand outlines]

[Shorthand outlines] x

[Shorthand outlines]

[Shorthand outlines]

[Shorthand outlines] x   (108)

3. *[Shorthand outlines]*

[Shorthand outlines]

[Shorthand outlines] x

[Shorthand outlines] x

[Shorthand outlines] x   (54)

APPENDIX

Principal Cities

New York

Chicago (Ill.)

Philadelphia (Pa.)

Detroit (Mich.)

Los Angeles (Calif.)

Cleveland (Ohio)

St. Louis (Mo.)

Baltimore (Md.)

Boston (Mass.)

Pittsburgh (Pa.)

San Francisco (Calif.)

Buffalo (N. Y.)

Milwaukee (Wis.)

Washington (D. C.)

New Orleans (La.)

Minneapolis (Minn.)

Cincinnati (Ohio)

Newark (N. J.)

Kansas City (Mo.)

Indianapolis (Ind.)

Seattle (Wash.)

Atlanta (Ga.)

Rochester (N. Y.)

Jersey City (N. J.)

Louisville (Ky.)

Portland (Ore.)

Denver (Colo.)

Houston (Texas)

Toledo (Ohio)

Oakland (Calif.)

Columbus (Ohio)

St. Paul (Minn.)

Dallas (Texas)

Birmingham (Ala.)

Akron (Ohio)

San Antonio (Texas)

Memphis (Tenn.)

Providence (R. I.)

Omaha (Nebr.)

Syracuse (N. Y.)

Dayton (Ohio)

Worcester (Mass.)

Oklahoma City (Okla.)

Youngstown (Ohio)

Grand Rapids (Mich.)

Fort Worth (Texas)

New Haven (Conn.)

or

Hartford (Conn.)

Hollywood (Calif.)

Nashville (Tenn.)

States and Territories

Alabama		Missouri	
Alaska		Montana	
Arizona		Nebraska	
Arkansas		Nevada	
California		New Hampshire	
Canal Zone		New Jersey	
Colorado		New Mexico	
Connecticut	*or*	New York	
Delaware		North Carolina	
District of Columbia		North Dakota	
		Ohio	
Florida		Oklahoma	
Georgia		Oregon	
Idaho		Pennsylvania	
Illinois		Rhode Island	
Indiana		South Carolina	
Iowa		South Dakota	
Kansas		Tennessee	
Kentucky		Texas	
Louisiana		Utah	
Maine		Vermont	
Maryland		Virginia	
Massachusetts		Washington	
Michigan		West Virginia	
Minnesota		Wisconsin	
Mississippi		Wyoming	

Short Forms

Arranged alphabetically

The number in parenthesis indicates the Chapter in which the word is presented.

A

a (4)
accord-ing (14)
acknowl-edge (15)
advantage (12)
advertise--ment-d (16)
all (9)
altogether (10)
an (4)
and (6)
any (5)
anything (9)
are (6)
as (8)
as is (9)

B

balance (12)
balanced (12)
be (1)
because (8)
become (18)
been (12)
behalf (12)
belief (11)

believe-d (11)
beyond (7)
build-ing (11)
but (1)

C

call (11)
called (11)
can (5)
cannot (12)
care (11)
cared (14)
certificate (15)
character (15)
circum-stance (16)
cold (11)
come (3)
commer-cial-ly (16)
could (10)

D

danger (17)
dear (11)
deliver-y--ed (11)

description (11)
different-ce (5)
difficult (12)
difficulty (12)
distin-guish-ed (18)
do (1)
doctor, Dr. (11)
dollar (4)
during (11)

E

English (17)
equal-ly (11)
equaled (11)
especial-ly (9)
everything (11)
exchange-d (17)
expect-ed (10)
eye (7)

F

familiar-ity (17)
February (10)
financial-ly (17)
first (9)
for (4)

from (11)

G

general-ly (12)
gentleman (12)
gentlemen (12)
give-n (3)
go (5)
gold (12)
govern-ed (16)
govern-
  ment (16)
great (12)
guard (12)

H

had (4)
hand (15)
has (8)
have (2)
he (7)
him (3)
himself (9)
his (8)
hour (6)
how (7)
however (11)

I

I (7)
immediate (15)
important-
  -ce (14)

impossible (14)
improve-d-
  -ment (14)
in (5)
income (18)
inconvenience-
  -t-ly (18)
individual-
  -ly (16)
influence (9)
influenced (9)
inform-ed (10)
informa-
  tion (13)
inscribe-d (16)
inscription (16)
inspect-ed-
  -ion (10)
instruction (16)
instructive (16)
insurance (10)
interest (15)
investiga-
  tion (13)
is (8)
is as (9)
it (1)
itself (9)

J

January (10)

K

knowledge (15)

L

language (9)
large (6)
largely (11)
larger (11)
largest (9)
liberty (11)

M

me (7)
member (11)
mere (11)
more (11)
mortgage-d
  (17)
most (9)
Mr. (11)
much (9)
myself (9)

N

near (11)
neglect-ed (17)
never (10)
neverthe-
  less (18)
New York (9)
next (9)
nor (11)
northern (12)
nothing (9)
November (10)
number-ed (11)

O

object-ed (13)
objection (13)
of (4)
on (4)
opinion (12)
opportu-
  nity (14)
organiza-
  tion (13)
organize-d (13)
ought (5)
our (6)
ourselves (9)
over (11)
owe (5)
owing (9)
own (11)
owner (11)

P

particular (14)
people (11)
pleasure (11)
practice-d (17)
principal-
  -ly (11)
principle (11)
probable-
  -ly-ility (16)
prospect (16)
public (13)
publication (13)

publish-ed (13)
put (5)

Q

quite (10)

R

rather (15)
regular (16)
remark-ed (11
remember-
  -ed (11)
represent-
  -ed (12)
represen-
  tative (12)
respect-ed (10
respectful-
  -ly (11)
responsi-
  ble-ility (12)

S

satisfaction (13
satisfactory (10
school (15)
schooled (15)
sent (10)
several (8)
shall (2)
short (15)
should (6)
significance (16)
significant (16)

signify-ied (16)
something (9)
southern (12)
speak (8)
special-ly (8)
spirit (15)
subject-ed (8)
sufficient-
  -ly-cy (16)
sure (11)
surprise (11)
surprised (11)

T

telegram (17)
tell (11)
thank-ed (6)
that (10)
the (1)
their (11)
them (2)
themselves (9)
there (11)
therefore (15)
thing (3)
think (2)
third (12)
this (8)
those (8)
though (9)
thus (8)
till (11)

to (1)

to be (5)

together (10)

told (12)

too (1)

toward (12)

trade (12)

tried (12)

truth (11)

two (1)

U

under (15)

United States (9)

university (17)

usual-ly (2)

V

very (11)

W

was (2)

we (3)

welcome (18)

what (7)

whatever (16)

when (7)

whenever (16)

whether (14)

which (1)

who (1)

whose (6)

why (7)

wish (5)

wished (10)

with (7)

within (12)

without (10)

wonderful-ly (15)

word (15)

would (7)

writer (15)

Y

yard (15)

year (6)

you (7)

young (9)

your (6)

yesterday (13)

Contractions

LIST ONE

The Short Forms given in the text are for words included in lists of the two thousand commonest words, and are therefore very frequently used. The following additional contractions will be found useful in high-speed writing. The words occur in lists of the ten thousand commonest words.

A

administration

administrative

administrator

appointment

arbitrary

arbitration

architect-ure-al

assignment

B

bankruptcy

C

capable

characteristic

contentment

D

dangerous

defective

deficient-ly-cy

democracy-atic

demonstrate

demonstration

destruction

discharge-d

E

efficient-ly-cy

electric

electrical

electricity

emergency

England

enlarge

enlargement

entertainment

enthusiastic-m

establish-ed-ment

executive

executor

expediency

expenditure

expensive

I

identical

identification

imperfect-ion-ly

incorporated

independent-ly-ce

indispensable-ly

influential-ly

intelligence

intelligent-ly

introduction

investment

irregular

J

jurisdiction

justification

L

legislative

legislature

M

manufacture-d

manufacturer

manuscript

mathematics

maximum

mechanical-ly

messenger

minimum

ministry

misfortune

monstrous

N

negligence

notwithstanding

O

objectionable

objective

P

passenger

peculiar-ity

perform-ed

performance

practicable

prejudice-d-ial-ly

preliminary

production

productive

project-ed

proportion-ed

prospective

publisher

Q

questionable-ly

R

reform-ed

remarkable-ly

representation

republic

republican

respective

respectively

S

selfish-ness

sensible-ly-ility

stranger

subscribe-d

subscription

substantial-ly

suspect-ed

sympathetic

T

telegraphic

thankful

U

unanimous-ly

uniform-ity-ly

universal

universe

V

valuation

Contractions

LIST TWO

(These words do not occur in lists of the ten thousand commonest words.)

A

abandonment
administrate
administratrix
amalgamate
amalgamation
arbitrate
arbitrator
attainment

C

circumstantial
contingency
cross-examination
cross-examine-d

D

denomination-al
destructive
destructively

E

enlarger
enlightenment
executrix
exigency
extinguish-ed

F

falsification
familiarization
familiarize

G

generalization

H

henceforward
howsoever

I

imperturbable
inconsiderate
informer
intelligible-ly
irrecoverable-ly
irremovable-ly
irrespective
irrespectively
irresponsible-ility

M

magnetic-ism
mathematical-ly
mathematician

metropolitan

O

obstruction
obstructive
oneself
organizer

P

performer
perpendicular
perspective
proficient-ly-cy
proportionate-ly
prospectus

R

recoverable
reformer
relinquish-ed
remonstrance
remonstrate
removable
reproduction

retrospect
retrospection
retrospective

S

signification
stringency
subjection
subjective

T

thenceforward

U

unanimity
universality
unprincipled

W

whensoever
whereinsoever
wheresoever
whithersoever

INDEX

The figures refer to the **paragraphs,** *except where the page is mentioned.*